Why
Suffering?

why
suffering?

*Finding Meaning and
Comfort When Life
Doesn't Make Sense*

RAVI ZACHARIAS
and
VINCE VITALE

New York   Boston   Nashville

Scripture quotations are taken from the Holy Bible, New International Version® NIV®, unless otherwise noted. Copyright © 1973, 1978, 1984, 2011 by Biblica, Inc.™ Used by permission of Zondervan. All rights reserved worldwide. www.zondervan.com. The "NIV" and "New International Version" are trademarks registered in the United States Patent and Trademark Office by Biblica Inc.™

Scripture quotations noted ESV are from The Holy Bible, English Standard Version, copyright © 2001 by Crossway Bibles, a publishing ministry of Good News Publishers. Used by permission. All rights reserved.

Scripture quotations noted KJV are from the King James Version of the Holy Bible.

Scripture quotations noted NLT are taken from the Holy Bible, New Living Translation, copyright © 1996, 2004, 2007, 2013 by Tyndale House Foundation. Used by permission of Tyndale House Publishers, Inc., Carol Stream, Illinois 60188. All rights reserved.

Scripture quotations noted NRSV are from the New Revised Standard Version of the Bible, copyright © 1989, by the Division of Christian Education of the National Council of the Churches of Christ in the United States of America. All rights reserved.

FaithWords
Hachette Book Group
1290 Avenue of the Americas
New York, NY 10104

www.faithwords.com

Printed in the United States of America

LSC-C

Originally published in hardcover by Hachette Book Group.
First trade edition: October 2015
10 9 8

FaithWords is a division of Hachette Book Group, Inc.
The FaithWords name and logo are trademarks of Hachette Book Group, Inc.

The Hachette Speakers Bureau provides a wide range of authors for speaking events. To find out more, go to www.hachettespeakersbureau.com or call (866) 376-6591.

The publisher is not responsible for websites (or their content) that are not owned by the publisher.

Library of Congress Cataloging-in-Publication Data

Zacharias, Ravi K.
    Why suffering? : finding meaning and comfort when life doesn't make sense / Ravi Zacharias and Vince Vitale.
        pages cm
    ISBN 978-1-4555-4970-2 (hardback) — ISBN 978-1-4789-3022-8 (audiobook) — ISBN 978-1-4789-8258-6 (audio download)   1. Suffering—Religious aspects—Christianity.   2. Pain—Religious aspects—Christianity.   I. Vitale, Vince.   II. Title.
    BV4909.Z33 2014
    231'.8—dc23
                                                                    2014019130

ISBN 978-1-4555-4969-6 (pbk.)

Ravi Zacharias: To James Riady and Mo Anderson: two very dear friends—brilliant in what they do, generous in how they give, candid in the failures through which they have come, committed totally to Jesus Christ whom they love and serve. I am most grateful for their love and friendship.

Vince Vitale: To Carla and Vincent Vitale—a mother with the strength to always see the good, a father with the courage to seek God in the bad, parents who in their love for me taught me to ground my life in a love that sacrifices for others. With love and gratitude beyond words, your son Vince

Contents

CHAPTER I

—§—

THE QUESTION

Ravi Zacharias

I grew up in a neighborhood in New Delhi, India, where communities defined friendships. Houses were close to one another, we played together with the neighborhood kids, and we often crossed one another's front or back yards on our way to the store or to school. It happened to be government employee housing, and so all the homes were identical inside and out. Our parents were all friends, and meals were often shared in each other's homes. There was never an issue of finding babysitters because either the servants in the house or the neighbors were there to meet the need. We knew one another's pay scale and place in society.

We also knew our neighbors' hurts. The pains that each bore were, in effect, community knowledge. I had a close friend who lived about six doors down, no more than a three-minute walk. Often I would cross his backyard as a shortcut to go to the neighborhood convenience store. His father was a good friend to my dad. When I was about fifteen years old,

I remember a scene that bothered me a lot but that I never quite understood. Each time I would cross my friend's yard, I could hear his father sobbing uncontrollably, muttering away some words of plea for hope. His wife would be there, sitting on the bed beside him, just stroking his back, oftentimes with tears running down her face.

I wondered what this was about, considering it was a common scene and an obviously disconcerting situation. I asked my friends what had happened and was told he'd had a "nervous breakdown." I had no clue what that was. I asked my mother to explain it. Knowing why I was asking, she simply said, "Something terrible must have happened and this man no longer has the ability to face life. His constant crying shows he cannot control the pain in his heart and the tears from his eyes."

I was quite young but was jolted on the inside: One could reach a stage where they could no longer control the pain in their heart and the tears from their eyes?

I thought about that often. Certainly, pain was a reality. I could not even get to the convenience store without having to admit that. The only difference seemed to be who controlled and faced it better, and why. How does one endure grief and pain? How does one manage it in life? Where do we go for answers when we suffer ourselves or when we see those we love suffering?

"A Baby's Funeral" is an essay by one of my favorite authors, the Englishman F. W. Boreham. He tells of a time as a younger minister when he looked out his window and saw an anxious woman walking back and forth in front of his home, but never quite making it to the doorway. So he stepped outside and asked if he could help her. She said she needed help from a minister, and asked if she could step in for a few minutes. So he ushered her in and she sat in his study looking terribly nervous and tongue-tied. She finally spoke up: "I have a newborn baby that has just died. I need a minister to perform the funeral."

Boreham asked several questions, took down the details, and said he would help in any way he could. She left and plans were made for the burial a couple of days from then. Boreham and his wife left after that conversation for a picnic that they had planned. But he couldn't get the woman's story out of his mind and said to his wife, "Something is not right. Her story just doesn't add up." They headed back home at dusk, and to their surprise, the woman was still pacing outside their home waiting for them to return. They invited her in.

"I have not told you the whole truth," she said. "Actually this baby was born illegitimately and deformed. She didn't live very long. I just want to give her an honorable burial with just her name on the stone." Boreham was deeply moved and the funeral was planned.

They arrived at the cemetery and he was surprised to find that nobody had been buried there before. It was pouring rain, and he and his wife, with this woman and the baby in a small casket, were all who were present at the burial. An illegitimate child, deformed, the first in a cemetery, under pouring rain—that was the funeral at which he officiated.

Years later Boreham took a train journey with a veteran bishop who was making stops to meet the pastors of small churches in the towns along the route. Boreham would stay a little distance away to let the bishop have some private time with these ministers. It was obvious that they were sharing the stories and challenges of ministering to people in their respective congregations. Boreham remembered well the closing words of the bishop in each instance: "Just be there for them...just be there for them in their need."

As he journeyed back that day, Boreham's thoughts returned to the woman with her baby. Years had gone by since that funeral, but every Sunday he could be certain of one face in his congregation. It was that woman. The first time he met her, her face was tearstained and her eyes fearful. As the years went by, the tears were wiped away and the eyes spoke of belonging to a message and a hope and a people that carried her through.

Seldom in one life do all forms of agony converge—a moral struggle, a heartbreak of grief, a little one at the heart of the story, the ultimate desolation of being buried in an empty cemetery, nature pouring its "tears" in a pounding rain, and yet the words of Scripture, the caring heart of a minister, and the years of belonging to a loving community all coming together in one life. What cradles a heart when such griefs converge? Somewhere in the community of those who have set their hope upon God, this woman found comfort and meaning amid the hardest question she ever had to face: Why suffering?

In each chapter of this book, my colleague Vince Vitale or I will outline a different response to this enormous question. Some of the chapters will take a fresh look at an ancient response. Others will propose new responses for your consideration. The responses are of course deeply related, but by looking at them separately we hope to show that the resources of the Christian community for approaching this ever-present challenge are both richer and more numerous than typically assumed.

The Challenge

Before we get to responses, though, I want to linger on the question—to hear it, to frame it, and to ask what it presupposes about who we are. This brings the question of suffering to a felt reality and, if properly addressed, gives us the prospect of hope. As for the intellectual side of this debate, I promise I will get to it. But first I would like to focus on where the darkness of evil and suffering hovers most and where the first glimmer of light may shine.

It is safe to say that both skeptic and believer alike share one opinion in common: The question of pain and suffering provides the greatest challenge to belief in God. In a discussion between scholars the issue of a world torn by suffering is often described as an insoluble *trilemma*. The argument by skeptics is positioned by first posing three basic claims that are adhered to by a Christian and then showing these claims to be irreconcilable. At least, they insist, these claims as they define them must be held by a Christian:

1. God is all-powerful: He can do anything He wills.
2. God is all-loving: He cares with an intense value for His creation.
3. Evil is a reality: Suffering is an all-pervading part of this world.

At face value, it is obvious that the ideas are indeed at variance. An all-powerful God can do anything He pleases, and from our perspective, the loving thing to do is to ease the pain of someone you love. Yet evil and suffering occupy a major part of our human experience; God has not removed them. These assertions together make no sense. This is the trilemma.

It is almost impossible to find any treatment of the subject without encountering this "obvious" incoherence. So the logical conclusion to solving the trilemma is that one or all three of these assertions must be denied. It is too obvious to deny that evil is a reality so, it is asserted, the Christian must surrender at least one of the first two beliefs and perhaps both—either God is not all-powerful, or He is not all-loving, or He is neither.

In fact, some philosophers go even further. Not only do they think that defending these three ideas as compatible is irrational, they believe that the problem is so acute that it makes belief in God irrational. It is no longer merely a defense that theism has to muster; it is an offense that makes theism a violation of reason.

Interestingly, the skeptic seldom pauses to go where the trilemma logically and ultimately leads philosophically; if the first two statements are denied, the most empirically evident statement—that evil is a reality—will ultimately have to be denied as well. But I shall not get ahead of myself here.

So compelling is this trilemma to the skeptic that it is often considered absolute proof of God's nonexistence. Killing God—what Nietzsche deemed the greatest deed—has been accomplished. Australian philosopher and strident atheist J. L. Mackie said it in these words:

> It can be shown, not that religious beliefs lack rational support, but that they are positively irrational, that the several parts of the essential theological doctrine are inconsistent with one another, so that the theologian can maintain his position as a whole only by a much more extreme rejection of reason than in the former case. He must now be prepared to believe, not merely what cannot be proved, but what can be *disproved* from other beliefs that he also holds.[1]

To Mackie, and to those who support his challenge, it is not so much a critique from a counter perspective that destroys Christian belief, but that these affirmations of belief within the Christian faith actually result in its own demise when put to the test of reason. So strongly is this argument held that it is branded the Evidential Argument from Evil, a counterpoint to theism.

When a counter to this charge of irrationality reveals the incoherence of the challenge, the question is suddenly repositioned. What do I mean by that? Take a look again at the three assertions.

1. God is all-powerful: He can do whatever He pleases.
2. God is all-loving: He cares for His creation.
3. Evil is a reality: Suffering is a real part of our human experience.

Each of these statements dies the death of a thousand qualifications: Who said that God can do anything He pleases and
what does that really mean? What does "He pleases" mean?
Can He do something that is mutually exclusive? Can He
make a square circle? Can He lie and state it as the truth?

The challenge is actually quite silly. If God can do anything, then He surely can even allow evil and call it good.
Why does He have to explain it? Surely, if omnipotence means
all-powerful without even logical or rational limitation, He
can allow evil to exist and not see any incoherence in it. And
if God can do anything He pleases why can't He simply be
incoherent as well? That may be irrational to the skeptic, but
does not limitless power also mean the power to be irrational
without justification?

Or take the second premise: Is eliminating pain always the
loving thing to do? Is it a quid pro quo that if you love somebody you will make their life totally free from pain? Taking it
a step further, does love always mean giving one the freedom
to have or do whatever one wishes? Is it love to remove boundaries? Very quickly one can see that every premise as stated
or implied by the critic makes assumptions that are actually
irrational.

That is why in debates the attacker quickly shifts the attack
in another direction: Why would God have created such a
world in the first place when in His omniscience He could
foresee the extent of evil that would be done and the depths
to which the innocent would suffer? By presenting it this
way, the emotions are stretched to the ultimate limit when
one delineates the extent of evil. Now the problem becomes
thorny. No thinking, caring person can simply stroke his or

her chin and say, "That's true, but it's unfortunately the way it is." The anguish has to be felt and it *is* felt, and that is why the question of suffering is raised in the first place.

But in demanding an answer for the reality of suffering, the questioner is looking for an emotionally satisfying answer as much or perhaps even more than for an intellectually fulfilling answer. A person falling off a high ladder understands that he will fall downward in the direction of the ground. There is no intellectual struggle there. But his *emotional* struggle is why the ladder was faulty in the first place or why he was not more careful.

Is the Trilemma Too Trivial?

The response to this whole series of challenges can be brief or it can be lengthy. Let me just pose a counter question: Is this trilemma a comprehensive set of affirmations? What if we interject just one more assertion into consideration that the Christian faith *also* makes—that "God is all-wise"? Is this really more of a *quadrilemma* than a trilemma? God is all-powerful, all-loving, and all-wise...and evil exists. Maybe even a *quintilemma*? God is all-powerful, all-loving, all-wise, and *eternal*...and evil exists *in time*.

Any one of these assertions can be defended on reason alone. Why is it that we finite, self-serving, time-constrained, so-often-wrong human beings think we have all the wisdom needed in which to castigate God and hold Him before the bar of *our* wisdom within *our* timetable? Is it simply not possible that though thinking we are operating in the light, we could really be operating in the dark? Is it not also possible that there are character lessons learned in adversity that could never be learned in any other way?

Take the simple illustration of a person so engrossed in the story while watching a movie that there has become a disjunction between the viewer and the viewed of unbelievable proportions. My mother-in-law is that kind of a viewer. She becomes so riveted by what she is watching that she actually starts talking to the actors in the movie: "Watch out, there's somebody standing behind the door!" "Don't go in...don't go in!"

I become so frustrated at times like these that I find myself telling her that not only does the actor in the movie know what is going to happen, his goal is to make her think that he doesn't know and she is falling for his ruse. What is more, this is not the first time he is walking into that room. He has done it again and again until the director determines that he does it well enough to make her think he doesn't know what lies behind the door. The storyteller hopes to cross the line between imagination and reality suspended in time. If we didn't believe in this disjunction, it would be the end of all theater.

But in a so-called "true story," based on facts, an actor plays a role that actually happened. In reality there was a time and a place where there was no actor, but rather the unfolding story of a person's life that was as real as life itself.

God, who exists in the eternal, in creating time and people, gives us the backdrop to the story and enough information so that we can know how this story will end. The true seeker after truth has enough clues to enable him or her to endure through time what is of eternal value, and see in reality and experience the triumph of truth over a lie, of love over selfishness. It is the ultimate triumph of the sacred over the profane. Neither is imaginary, and neither can be explained without the reality of the other.

Several years ago, there was a powerful movie titled *Not Without My Daughter*. It is based on the real-life story of an American woman who married a Muslim man in the United States. After several years of happy marriage, the man took his wife and young daughter to Iran, his homeland, on a vacation. But it wasn't long before his wife realized that he had never planned to return to the United States but to keep at least his daughter in his homeland, even if his wife was able to leave. The story is full of high drama, emotion, and heart-wrenching struggle as the mother experiences the heartache of living with lies and of seeing her daughter raised in a culture with which she is not comfortable, facing hostility and abuse herself.

Gradually, she begins to lay a plan to smuggle her daughter out of Iran. With the help of some locals and with incredible risk, they begin their journey of escape. As the plan painstakingly succeeds, the final scene of the movie is of the mother staggering along an unfamiliar street with her daughter in her arms, not even sure where she is. When she hears something flapping in the wind, she looks up toward the sound and sees an American flag waving above a building. Suddenly, she realizes she is standing before an American embassy, and the tears stream uncontrollably down her cheeks; she has caught the scent and sight of freedom and of home.

I am convinced that such is the hope and victory of one

who grasps God's story for humanity. You arrive at the place of freedom to hope again, because you sense the very presence of the One who makes you free.

The Pain of Painlessness

Some time ago I read an interview with a woman who had a daughter with a rare medical condition. In the last line of the interview she said, "My prayer for my daughter every night is, 'Dear God, please let my daughter be able to feel pain.'" If that were all one read of the interview, what would be concluded? At best, our most beneficent thoughts would be that perhaps this child was callous and totally indifferent to anyone else's suffering, and the mother was praying that her daughter would learn to empathize with others by experiencing pain herself. But that was not the case. The daughter she spoke of suffered from a rare medical condition that made it impossible for her to feel physical pain.

In a totally different narrative, even as I write the news is hot on the wires of a young Australian student in America gunned down by three young men whose sole motive was to kill for "the fun of it." No pain over what they had done, no remorse, no guilt. The father of one of them said, "My son doesn't feel the weight of doing anything wrong."

Here are two instances of a painless existence. But the difference between them is huge. In the first instance a child was born with a rare congenital disease called CIPA (congenital insensitivity to pain with anhidrosis). This horrific disease has stricken only very few people in human history. The body simply does not feel pain, but this does not mean that the body cannot be wounded. In fact, therein lies the danger: The girl could step on a rusty nail that penetrated her foot and consequently develop a life-threatening infection, but she would feel no pain and not even realize that she had been wounded. She could place her hand on a burning stove and not feel the flesh melt.

In other words, there are two realities. There is actual destruction and debilitation without a concomitant felt loss, because there is an actual loss at a deeper level on which the signal system to the body is no longer functioning. This is a physical malady of deadly proportions; thus the mother's prayer, "Please let my daughter feel pain."

The second instance, that of the killing of a man for the fun of it, is actually an even more deadly malady, because here pain is inflicted without any emotional response. In a civilized society it is expected that someone who inflicts pain should feel remorse and anguish over the deed. What a terrifying world this would be if each of us had a neighbor of such deformity that though a perpetrator of pain, they themselves felt none. They could hurt us for "the fun of it."

Why is it that while the former situation is equally instructive, the latter is more terrifying? Both tell us that pain is a real indicator for a better purpose, and both tell us that when an underlying malfunction is real, the symptomatic issues, though secondary, are warning lights of what needs to be fixed. The worst kinds of diseases are the ones where there are no symptoms that indicate the fatal effect is doing its deadly work.

Imagine you are taking a path that zigzags up a hill, rather than running straight up, because of the steep angle of the climb. As you climb, at times you seem to be moving farther away from your destination at the top because you are angling across the mountain rather than going straight up. Yet in reality you are actually moving closer to the top all the time.

Add to this one further component, that it is also true that the shortest distance to a destination is not always the best route because the most important experiences are often missed. One can quickly see how our journeys in life contain ready examples of traveling toward the destination we seek along a path that is not always free from impediments or obstructions or pain, and that often this is the better way to go. Freedom from pain is not the only indicator of whether or not something is beneficial.

The Reasoning of Reason

Philosophers like J. L. Mackie who use the existence of evil as an argument against God fail to differentiate between logic and reasoning. A person using the same logic as Mackie does can apply a different reasoning to the same situation and come up with a totally different conclusion.

I am from India. There is an old Indian popular song that says:

> My shoes are Japanese, these trousers English;
> The red cap on my head, Russian, yet my heart is Indian.[2]

Of course, "heart" here refers to the way one thinks and feels. The problem of suffering is felt in the East as much as it is felt in the West. Pain is the same East or West; where one lives and the culture from which one comes are inconsequential. Both mourn their dead, both visit loved ones in hospitals, both have pain management clinics and psychotherapists. And when the Muslim says "Insha Allah," or the Hindu mutters "kismet" (luck), or the Buddhist "karma," they understand the trilemma we are talking about, though their reasoning process is not the same as Mackie's and those who pose this trilemma as "insoluble." Of course I am not talking about those in villages who have never heard of Leibniz or Augustine. I am talking about the educated and those well-versed in philosophy, even Western philosophy.

Using logic as a test for truth and reasoning does not always result in the same implications of what is true. Worldviews must be put through the sieve of our reasoning process to examine if we have done justice to the facts and to logic or have merely forced conclusions from them that amputate other realities. Such extrapolations are often tendentious and reveal more of the cultural bias from which the contender argues.

If one is to be fair to all the major positions, one must test the logic of one's own position before indiscriminately disposing of an alternative position. Declaring a conundrum insoluble by a crass sterile logic that fails to fully examine the affirmations runs the risk of being illogical and unreal. It is imperative that we understand not only the logical problem that is being presented but the reasoning process that we are bringing to bear upon this very important question.

In a recent interview philosopher Daniel Dennett described Alvin Plantinga's defense of Christian theism in the context of the problem of evil as "logically impeccable [yet] preposterous."[3]

That's quite a statement. I am assuming that by "logically" here he not only means that Plantinga's argument has explanatory power but that it is coherent, as that is a necessary component of being logical. What, then, does he mean by preposterous? He must mean only that in his view *any* justification of evil is preposterous. So now he has inevitably shifted to making a value judgment.

In that same interview, Dennett speaks strongly against anyone who believes in absolutes. One can only ask him if he holds that position absolutely, but we won't stop his argument that quickly. If Plantinga's position is logical yet preposterous, does that mean that Dennett's own position on evil is therefore illogical but not preposterous, or in fact both illogical and preposterous? Whatever we conclude, from the theistic viewpoint the trilemma can be invoked only in the context and within the constrictions of time, and therefore Christian belief can be logically sustained.

The View from Brokenness

Some months ago, a friend of mine arranged for me to have the privilege of visiting and speaking to prisoners at the infamous Angola prison in Louisiana, once known as the most dangerous prison in America. There are about five thousand inmates in Angola, more than 85 percent of whom are serving life without parole and forty-five of whom are on death row. Not very many years ago when a prisoner was processed into Angola he was given a knife to protect himself. It was not uncommon to see bloodstains on the floors and walls. These are among the toughest and meanest criminals you could meet. Entering that prison for life without parole was to say good-bye to civility, with no possibility of freedom.

Things have changed at Angola. I couldn't help but wonder, as I met some of the prisoners and was able to talk with them one-on-one, what crimes they had committed and what had caused this apparently calm and mild-mannered person to do whatever he had done that landed him here. I spoke in the prison seminary, in which about ninety prisoners are enrolled at a time. Afterward, I was chatting with a handful of men and one of them told me a little bit about his past and how he ended up in Angola for life without parole. I asked him, "How do you handle the prospect that you will never get out of here, and that this is where your life will now be spent?"

He looked to me to be a man no older than his mid-thirties. He answered, "You know, sir, if you knew the kind of person I was before I came here, and what I have now become because of the freedom Jesus Christ has brought to my soul, I can only say that if this is what it took to bring me to my senses, I am happy to spend the rest of my life here." Then he paused and said, "Please pray for my parents. They think they are free, but they are in a prison of their own darkness without God."

That evening it was all I could do to fight back the tears as I watched this same man leading more than seven hundred prisoners in worship before I spoke. It was one of the most sobering experiences I have ever had. A hard-core criminal who has experienced redemption conveys a powerful story of how deep the human malady is, and that often one must be brought very low before acquiring the ability to understand what lies beneath evil.

A good friend of mine is a professional comedian, one of the most successful stand-up comics of all time. I mention this because few know the depths of this man's commitment to make the world a better place. Making people laugh is his avocation; giving people hope is his real passion. In a recent conversation he spoke of his favorite day of the week: the day he leads a Bible study for the homeless in Atlanta, Georgia. He told me of a man who had been banished from his family for twenty-two years. Any attempt he made to go back home was rebuffed because his family members felt they could not trust him.

One day my friend was teaching the story of the prodigal son in the Bible study. This man pondered the story for some time, rereading it and studying it carefully. "You know what?" he finally said to my friend. "There is a world of difference between saying 'I have made a mistake' and saying 'I have sinned.' A huge difference! When the son in the parable goes back to his father, he doesn't say, 'I have made a mistake.' He says 'I have sinned against heaven and against you.'"

Not long after coming to terms with the implications of the prodigal's return, this homeless man also returned home to his mother and said to her, "I have stolen from you, I have deceived you, I have lied to you. I have sinned against heaven and against you. I ask your forgiveness for my sin." Twenty-two shattered years and then the discovery of a most basic truth. He didn't expect any change in his family's attitude toward him; he just wanted them to know that he understood what he had done to them and to ask for their forgiveness.

The family, seeing for the first time that he viewed his actions in such self-revealing terms, swung open the doors of their hearts and their house and asked him to come home. He is back with his family. But every week he returns to this Bible study for the homeless to tell the story of his own journey back to God. "I have sinned." Those words are from the depths of remorse that is rightly felt.

Where Definitions Begin

As I begin this discussion, let me state why I believe that the atheistic position breeds more rational dissonance than so-called evidence against God. One has to start off with a simple question: Is there a moral framework to life? Are the moral judgments we make reflective of a reality that is not just a preference of values but is in some nature binding upon us? You see, to the naturalist, the presence of evil is troubling with a double edge. From where do they even get the category of evil? And second, how do they break its stranglehold?

To the Christian theist, good and evil have a point of reference. With the naturalistic starting point, good and evil are either emotionally sensed or pragmatically driven, both of which fall victim to the reasoning processes of our diverse cultures. This is a glaring inconsistency within naturalism.

Some time ago I was watching a BBC documentary titled *Our Planet Earth*. It is a fascinating series dealing with the marvel and the mystery of life on this planet we call Earth. It is very difficult to watch and not be intrigued by the intricate forms of life and how they relate to one another. From deep within caves where only a handful of humans have ever descended to the rigors of frigid polar survival seen through the lens of a camera and the almost clownish walk of penguins, I watched in amazement.

The hardest part of the program to view is the search-and-devour instinct of the birds and beasts as each finds its victim, and then becomes the victim of another. I remember reading the words of Voltaire as he mused on the predatory chain of life, how the miseries of each are supposed to make up the good of all, and of Tennyson's words in *In Memoriam*: "Nature, red in tooth and claw..."[4] It is hard to escape the tragedy of it and not ask the question of why it must be so.

In this particular program, watching the majestic polar bear, there was one scene in particular that left me with torn emotions. These magnificent, fearsome creatures that survive in temperatures that would freeze the human body within minutes are at once beautiful and savage. The polar bear has a task at hand. He has to find food. He is limited by a body that hasn't eaten in weeks and is at its weakest, and by a thinning ice surface that will soon crumble under his weight as the spring thaw progresses. So the male moves at a determined clip as quickly and carefully as he can. The ice is melting and cannot support his weight so he has to measure his steps while time is at a premium.

He soon comes upon a pod of walruses and stops to rest and plan his attack. He knows that his best bet are the newborn babies, the weakest in the pack, but his challenge is to break through the ring of adult walruses and the protective instinct of the parents, who will be guarding their babies against an attacker. He makes his move. He climbs atop one parent and tries desperately to incapacitate it so that he has access to the baby. But the rest of the herd use their weight and their tusks to fight him off. Clumsy as they appear, they are able to strike into the flesh of the bear. Their own thick coats are hard to chew through and their tusks can inflict lethal wounds upon the attacker.

The polar bear makes one last savage swipe with his paw but fails. On the verge of giving up, he sees another opening into the pack and bounds over to exploit that. This time he is atop the mother of a little baby in a battle of life or death for both the bear and the walruses. Try as he does, exhausted in his weakened state by his attempts he simply cannot overpower the resistance and protective instinct of the adult walruses.

There was a struggle of my own emotions as I watched the bear try to grab the little one and when it failed, turn around and collapse, succumbing to his own wounds. The last scene was the bear struggling to stand, clawing at the ice and digging his own grave.

The commentator added in somber tones that the death of this polar bear is a picture of the diminishing population of the species and of the real possibility of their extinction, and is caused by global warming for which human beings are responsible.

What a fascinating study, incredible assumptions, awe-inspiring filming demanding a measured and sober response to the world of nature. Really? Is that what the program was all about? Or is there something more tugging at the human soul? Why a world order such as this? Why the appeal to beauty, to majesty, and then to the responsibility of humanity? If it was just about saving the bear, a simple solution would be to leave dead animals within reach of the hungry animals so that when famished they would have all they needed. What is the paradigm that best fits this scenario and countless others like it? Was the documentary really about saving polar bears or was it about the responsibility of humanity for the world in which we live?

The BBC commentator could not resist making a moral application, appealing to the emotions and consciences of the viewers and highlighting our responsibility for the demise of the polar bear population. Why did the bears not get into a huddle before sending the father on the mission to find food and discuss whether the walrus population also had rights? Why did the mother bear not say to the papa bear, "We protect our own cubs even to the point of death. Do you think you're being fair to go after another animal's baby?" Was there any stir of conscience in the bears before going on the kill? No. We do not expect the creaturely world to act except by natural instinct. They are not moral creatures. They are beasts that live to survive and nothing else matters.

If we are naturalists, why do we expect the human species to be any different and to react with moral reasoning? Why should it bother us when someone says, "I really don't care about anyone or anything else; I want to live my lifestyle"? Oscar Wilde once said that we don't appreciate sunsets because we don't have to pay for them. G. K. Chesterton remarked that Wilde was wrong: "We can pay for them by not being Oscar Wilde."[5]

Do you see how deep the questions really lie? To believe that by solving one simple environmental dilemma we've answered the questions of existence is like believing that just because we understand gravity we will have the moral rea-

THE QUESTION • 23

soning not to push somebody off the roof. Everyone knows that dropping bombs kills people, but that hasn't kept us from going to war. We must still answer the question of why it is wrong to murder.

Frankly, I didn't have to see the documentary to have that surge of emotions and caring for the animal world. I have had the privilege of driving in an open vehicle through one of South Africa's most beautiful safari regions, hoping to see the "big five"—the lion, the leopard, the buffalo, the rhinoceros, and the elephant. One night we witnessed the rare sight, even for the safari guides, of three lions and their cubs feasting upon the carcass of a dead elephant. How the elephant had been felled the guides would not hazard a guess. It is apparently not common for a lion to attack an elephant.

As we approached them, some fifteen feet from their banquet, the lions just gave us the eye with a look that eloquently conveyed, "Don't you dare come any nearer." Hiding nearby were the hyenas, and perched above the trees were the vultures, each waiting their turn. We gladly honored that look. Wouldn't it have been nicer of the lions to have said to the hyenas and vultures, "Come on over, there's plenty here for all of us."

We don't expect that of animals, but as humans we do ask those who have plenty to share with those who have none; in fact, moral reasoning is what helps to meet the needs of the deprived. Why do we expect a different standard of ourselves than of the beasts? Is it not because we see the creaturely kingdom in its splendor as wild and without moral debate?

In fact, just a few hundred feet from where we were

watching was an elephant stripping the bark from a tree with its trunk; having fed itself, it would leave the tree to die. Scores of trees bore the scars of an elephant's visit. It is humanity that is replenishing those trees so that the beasts can survive. In this mix of life and death and destruction the problem of pain stares at us daily. What is the explanation if naturalism is all there is? Is there a story that is true and comprehensive in dealing with the facts?

The Flowers and the Thorns

Now let me shift the scene from the actual to the imagined. Do you remember the old parable of the gardener framed by Antony Flew and John Wisdom?[6] In the parable two explorers come upon a scene where they find a well-cleared area with beautiful flowers growing among thorns. A debate ensues as to whether or not there is a gardener. One argues that there has to be a gardener or there is no way to explain the beauty and arrangement of the flowers. The other counters that there couldn't be a gardener or he would have pulled out the weeds and the thorns that were in danger of choking the flowers.

So they wait and watch and see no one. The conclusion is drawn that they have seen no gardener and, therefore, there is no gardener; the garden just functions according to some natural law that permits both flowers and weeds to flourish. For, they ask, what is the difference between an imaginary gardener and no gardener at all?

John Frame, another philosopher, writes his own parable

built on the same evidence.[7] But in his parable there is a gardener who is seen and there are footprints, evidence of his existence. At the end of his parable he asks the skeptic, What is the difference between an imaginary gardener and a garden with flowers that could have been planted only by a real gardener?

Both parables end in a question. Which parable truly answers the evidence and the questions?

In the East there is a story of a lion going from animal to animal asking each one who is king of the forest. One after another they all bow before him and say, "You are, O lion!" Finally the lion meets up with an elephant and asks the same question. In response the elephant wraps its trunk around the lion, lifts it up high into the air, and then slams it to the ground. The lion gets to its feet, somewhat shaken, and says, "You don't have to get so upset...I just asked you a simple question."

So it is that I ask a simple question of the naturalist: Since you say that the reality of evil causes you, a human being, to disbelieve in God, what is your definition of being human? Are we merely educated animals, different to the animal world only in degree, in which case there is no reason for us to act any differently than the animals, and evil as a category cannot exist? Or are we *essentially* different, equipped with a sense of moral responsibility that is inescapable and subject to a different set of rules?

Before anything is lived it has to be believed, and not everything that is believed is always lived out. The reality is that the disavowal of belief in God is fraught with immense logical and existential problems. If indeed the existence of God (from which the essential nature of man derives) is denied, three logical conclusions must follow.

1. Man (humanity) becomes God.
2. The body becomes the soul.
3. Time becomes eternity.

I have given this outline as simply stated. I will explain it at greater length later. For now, these implications are fairly obvious: Can we live with their ramifications? What becomes of the problem of evil if these implications are true?

Other religions attempt to answer these questions in their own terms, and atheists struggle to hold on to the categories they have invented. Christianity suggests that coherent and livable responses are to be found not in humanity becoming God, but in the God who became human. Vince and I will explore all of these possibilities in the ensuing chapters.

The Intellectual and the Pastoral

One more distinction should be emphasized from the outset. At least as important as the question of why there is suffering is the question of how we will face the pain.

The philosopher Alvin Plantinga knows this subject well, and in his book *God, Freedom, and Evil*, he applies penetrating philosophical scrutiny to the problem of suffering from his breadth of knowledge and depth of understanding. In the light

of that, I believe his statement below to be extremely perceptive and to have profound implications:

> In the presence of his own suffering or that of someone
> near to him he may find it difficult to maintain what he
> takes to be the proper attitude towards God. Faced with
> great personal suffering or misfortune, he may be tempted
> to rebel against God, to shake his fist in God's face, or
> even to give up belief in God altogether. But this is a prob-
> lem of a different dimension. Such a problem calls, not for
> philosophical enlightenment, but for pastoral care.[8]

That statement sums up the practical side of this question,
which is far different from the philosophical side of it, and
he is right on. I meet this need everywhere I travel. I have
known this need numerous times in my life. Where do we
find shepherding care as we walk through the valley of evil
and suffering?

In my opinion, one of the most meaningful books written on the problem of suffering is *Suffering and the Goodness
of God*. The editors, Christopher W. Morgan and Robert A.
Peterson, have done a brilliant job of pulling together some
of the finest scholarship to address various dimensions of the
problem.

To be sure, the scholars have a good understanding of
both the philosophical and the pastoral side of it. And after
all the different aspects concerning pain and suffering have
been covered, the last chapter is by philosopher theologian
John Feinberg, from whom I had the privilege of taking a

few courses while at graduate school. John Feinberg did his doctoral work at the University of Chicago, much of it on the subject at hand. He refers to his personal experience around pain and suffering in the following paragraph:

> I was raised around people who suffered greatly; my mother had one physical problem after another and this in part sparked my interest at an early age in the problem of pain and suffering. In seminary, I wrote my master of divinity thesis on Job...My doctoral dissertation even focused on the problems of evil and led to my book *The Many Faces of Evil*. If anyone had thought about this and was prepared to face affliction, surely it was I.[9]

Still, with all that theoretical knowledge he was unprepared for the suffering and pain he himself would have to endure. After he recounts what he went through, he says that his experience in the presence of pain and the intellectual answers to the problem of pain he had found were of no help to him when he was suffering himself: "The emotional and psychological pain was unrelenting, and the physical results from the stress and mental pain were devastating."[10]

How can that be? What transpired in his life between the intellectual answers and his own pain and suffering? On November 4, 1987, everything changed for him and his family when his wife was diagnosed with Huntington's disease. Huntington's disease is a genetically transmitted disease involving the premature deterioration of the brain. The symptoms of Huntington's disease are both physical and psychological. Physically, it means the gradual loss of control of all voluntary bodily movement; psychologically, it means memory loss and depression, and, as it progresses, the possibility of hallucinations and paranoid schizophrenia. A slowly developing disease, the symptoms do not become evident until about the age of thirty, and over the next ten to twenty years it is fatal. Worse for John and his wife, Pat, only one parent needs to carry the gene for Huntington's disease to be passed on to their child. They have three children, each born with a 50 percent chance of eventually receiving the same diagnosis as their mother.

It is difficult to read about the agony he has felt over his wife and the fear for his children, but his chapter in the book is worth reading. The emotions swing from one extreme to another and detail a classic example of how deep this struggle can be and how remote intellectual answers can be, even though they are important. Feinberg admits that when it came right down to it, what he needed was not the intellectual answers he already had but the pastoral care that Plantinga talks about.

Here the simple thought from Chesterton rings so powerfully: When belief in God becomes difficult, the tendency is to turn away from him—but in heaven's name to what? When Jesus asked the twelve disciples closest to Him whether they too would desert Him with the rest of His disciples, Peter replied for all of us down through the ages when he said, "Lord, to whom shall we go?" (John 6:68). Where can one go for an answer?

John Feinberg traced his journey through this maze and eventually arrived at the same truths he held earlier, but along the way he realized how fraught with perilous pitfalls the road to those conclusions was. For the first time he personally experienced the destructiveness of sin in the human experience and how critical it is to have the right counsel as you walk a lonely road. He has demonstrated it in his life and cautions Christians against giving glib answers to those in the midst of suffering and unpacks the foundational truths that have carried him through his valley.

This is where the Christian message stands tall above any other teaching on pain and suffering and goes beyond any other answers to our problem. The intellectual answers are important. But intellect alone cannot help us navigate the minefield of pain and suffering. Other worldviews also offer intellectual answers. But Christianity alone offers a person.

In the chapters ahead, Vince and I suggest that the resources of Christianity provide a wide range of helpful responses to the question, "Why suffering?" The strength of these responses is to be found not in pitting one against another but in appreciating their cumulative force, and in recognizing that a challenge as personal as the challenge of suffering requires responses varied enough to bring meaning and comfort to each particular circumstance and, most importantly, to each particular person.

Ideas cannot bring lasting meaning, comfort, or hope. Only a person can. At the core of every one of the responses we will offer is relationship with God—the freedom to enter into that relationship and the empowerment to live in the fullness of life that only that relationship provides.

CHAPTER 2

—§—

A RESPONSE OF FREEDOM

Ravi Zacharias

It happens that I am in Indonesia writing this chapter. I just spent a remarkable hour with a noted Christian leader, a man of multiple talents and gifts, in his later years. He asked me what I was writing on these days and when I told him I was writing on the problem of suffering his immediate answer was, "Suffering is necessary. It is impossible to live a complete life without suffering." There's the Eastern mind for you. I smiled. He continued, "If life is to be fully understood and lived, suffering is necessary." I was on the verge of another smile but instead asked, "How does one get to that place of belief without losing faith and certainty?"

As we talked further he told me his story. He is a Chinese gentleman and was raised from the time he was a toddler by a single mother who had been widowed early and raised eight children. I just shook my head as his story unfolded. He knew suffering. He had stared it in the eye from the time he was a child. He had a story. He had a metanarrative, that is, a larger picture into which his life was securely positioned by the love of his mother. Today he is the pastor of one of the largest churches in that country. Included in the church complex is an art museum and a state-of-the-art concert hall that features performances by the finest artists of the works of great composers such as Bach, Handel, Beethoven, and others. He himself is an accomplished conductor. For years he has preached every week in four countries. Every week.

I looked at him in his small cluttered study where we were having a simple lunch of chicken and rice and I marveled at the accomplishments of a man like this. His life was an answer to suffering. He found the combination of a Savior and the Creator of the world of beauty and hope. Implicit in this pastor's answer were three components: an argument, a story, and an application. His answer to me went straight for the application: "Suffering is necessary for life to be complete." But the argument and the story are in need of being presented and told every day in someone's life.

The Author of Life

I want to take you now through a simple progression of thought that reveals the primacy of human freedom in the Christian understanding of suffering.

The first and most important point is that God is the author of life. I do not wish to get bogged down in this point because there are other books that deal with the role of a Creator more thoroughly. But knowing that for many this is where it begins or ends, I should at least touch briefly upon it.

My colleague and friend John Lennox, professor at Oxford University, has written a powerful book titled *Seven Days That Divide the World*, in which he presents what I feel is the most plausible explanation of the Christian claim on creation and where the limitations lie for its defenders and challengers.[1] The bottom line is whether the world contains within itself scientifically tenable arguments to explain who we are and why we are here. That is a big question and the variant understandings of how it happened are numerous.

Often, what is presented as the ultimate cause is nothing more than an intermediary one. For Stephen Hawking to boast that gravity explains everything is simply ludicrous. It is not a credit to his scientific mind to posit such weak statements as sufficient explanation. That is no more an explanation than saying that the printing of a dictionary is explained by the existence of an alphabet.

The breadth of differences of opinion on how it happened is vast in the scientific community. For example, world-recognized Sri Lankan astronomer Chandra Wickramasinghe unshakably believes in the panspermian theory, which suggests that spores from the clouds or another planet seeded the earth. That's how it all began.

In an interview on the occasion of his retirement, Wickramasinghe talked of how he was mocked when he first came to that conclusion. He readily admitted that it was his colleague, Sir Frederick Hoyle, who came to his rescue, and suddenly his theory was given recognition. He and Hoyle were later awarded the Dag Hammarskjöld Gold Medal for Science, and the theory of panspermia has become mainstream in the new science of astrobiology—a link between astronomy and biology. The interview with him in the *Asian Tribune* is worth reading.[2]

I point this out to demonstrate that the existing theories are not monolithic and change constantly, as every discipline seeks footage in trying to find an explanation for how we got here. The reason they keep probing for a life-form on other planets is because our scientific laws do not explain origin of life. They may explain process but not origin.

The good news for the panspermian theorists is that the next time someone is accused of having his head in the clouds, he may have received the highest compliment. To add to it, these days all our conversations are stored in the cloud as well. So, one way or another, it may please some to learn that it all began up there rather than in a swamp. And if perchance our thinking does originate in a swamp, it still is stored in the cloud. The debate among naturalists goes on from the swamps of Africa to the clouds above us to the gravity that keeps us on the ground.

The American poet Henry Longfellow said:

> *Life is real! Life is earnest!*
> *And the grave is not its goal;*
> *Dust thou art, to dust returnest,*
> *Was not spoken of the soul.*[3]

The panspermianist will modify this to say:

> *Life is real! Life is earnest!*
> *And the grave is not its goal;*
> *Cloud thou art, to cloud returnest,*
> *Was indeed the essence of your soul.*

By the way, Wickramasinghe also believes that we are "mere decades" away from meeting life from other planets. All this to say that the theories of origin proposed by scientists run the gamut from how our values "biologized" to how our origins are "astrobiologized." In humility we had better recognize that the vastness of knowledge is still far from our grasp. There is still a blank sheet before the naturalists.

It has always been interesting to me that when Job cried out to God for answers to his pain and suffering in the book of Job, God began His personal response by going back to the beginning of time, asking Job how much he knew about how things came to be. "Where were you when I laid the earth's foundation?" (Job 38:4) God asked and then moved directly to the created order. The point is clear that if God is the author of life, He has an answer to suffering. If something indeed came from nothing then nothing is really the answer to suffering. But if we are the creation of a personal, moral, infinite, loving God, then He will have the answer for us.

Through the ordeal of losing everything he had except his life, Job found that all he needed to know was to keep his feet on the ground and his mind *above* the clouds. It was through the valley of his darkest nights and fears that he labored for his answers.

Many Voices, Same Destination

In the opening chapter of the excellent book *Suffering and the Goodness of God*, to which I have already drawn attention, Robert Yarbrough covers a lot of ground in unpacking the various responses that Christians give to the "Why?" of it all. In a brief but comprehensive manner he gives eleven different theses as to the "hows" and the "whys."[4]

Regardless of the how, for the Christian the starting point is that God is the author of life. So the difference really lies in one of two beginnings:

1. In the beginning God…with a purpose, with intent, with design, with a revealed blueprint, brought the created order into being; or

2. in the beginning nothing…no purpose, no design, yet from primordial slime or cloudburst with no prevision, nothing became something and the something gradually moved up the scale of complexity until thought emerged and, finally, this self-caused entity we call homo sapiens.

In the beginning was matter, or in the beginning was the mind of God? From these two starting points we have to understand why evil and suffering exist, why we hurt, bleed, suffer, and die.

Why God?

The argument that God is the author of life is presented with three assumptions:

1. Nothing physical in this universe explains its own existence.
2. Wherever one sees intelligibility, one assumes intelligence.
3. God has intervened in history and in moral reasoning.

Who, then, is the Creator? In the Christian worldview, He is the nonphysical, intelligent, moral, and personal first cause of the universe who, in the incarnation of Jesus Christ, revealed Himself to mankind. If science struggles to explain life and if attempted explanations require billions of years to transpire, the least we can do is give the Christian the same privilege of eternity and of the nonphysical to build a coherent worldview.

My father-in-law often talked of his older brother, who, when they were children, never liked to take responsibility for anything. On one occasion he inadvertently sat on a stack of what used to be called gramophone records...old LPs as we used to call them, the prehistoric version of CDs. Anyhow, he inadvertently sat on the stack and in one careless moment broke his father's treasured collection. He knew he was going to get his due.

Later that evening, when his dad came back from the office and saw the carnage still visible on the living room sofa, he stopped, stared, and bellowed out, "Who did this?" With a deadpan face Arnold said, "It got sat upon." Of course, I wasn't in existence at the time of the conversation, but I can only imagine what transpired during the interrogation. "It got sat upon!" What brilliant evasive thinking for a youngster! There was clearly an "it" that didn't explain its own origin. There was an instrument—a person involved—but he is conveniently removed by just talking of the action.

Such is the explanation of some in the world of the sciences. "It got acted upon." Even grammar is in question when one talks of "evolutionary wisdom," attributing rational thought to a predicate without a subject. From whence came the "it"?

The possibility of any other participant is ignored because to admit that there was one would be to admit that the "it" did not cause itself. With God as the prime mover, an explanation for everything else can be found. G. K. Chesterton said that the sun is the one created thing we cannot look at, but it is the means by which we look at the rest of creation. Like the sun, it is the spiritual that gives light to and explains everything else.[5]

What Is the Story?

Since it is most logical that God is the author, the inference is that there is a story. There is a script. In the last chapter I asked whether there is a story that is true and comprehensive in dealing with the facts of evil and suffering. I believe that there is, and this story has a beginning and a culmination point: *worth* and *worship*.

These terms are tied into love and forgiveness, which in turn are undergirded by the gift of freedom. But let's stay with worth and worship for now. Those two simple words summarize the story. This really should not be surprising. We all seek essential worth right from the time we can relate and express. Watching a child grow up and watching a child go wrong is often all about self-image and self-esteem. Belonging and value are not just characteristics of things; they are first characteristics of people. Life has essential value. Every life has worth, imbued with the image of God.

But in that essential worth, we have the responsibility to understand the Creator's design and purpose. That purpose is to enjoy the true nature of love and relationship, which are to be found only in Him. All other loves and relationships are meant to be a reflection of that perfect love and relationship.

Love has its boundaries and was never meant to be cheap. Love comes at the greatest cost and, when the cost is paid, brings the greatest reward. Watching a young bride and groom make their pledge to each other is not love. It is the promise of love and hope. Watching an elderly couple walk through a botanical garden hand in hand is love—the promise has been kept and the honor expressed. It is the same with God. Love is not when we first trust Him. Love is when through the vicissitudes of life we still trust Him, because we know God has kept His word to sustain us, come what may.

If worth and worship are in the design, brokenness and selfishness are part of the malady.

I remember a young woman once saying to me through her tears, "Let no one ever tell you that divorce is easy. It is the ultimate form of inner shattering." She went on to explain how many are hurt in the process. Does it happen? Yes. Is it painful? Yes. Why? Because it means the shattering of hope and of love. A broken love means a broken life. Love enters the deepest recesses of who we are. When love is plundered, the loneliness one is left with is agonizing. Are there some who will someday turn the corner? Thankfully, yes. But none will deny the sorrow of the past.

Why did we walk away from the love of God? We made a free choice. We divorced Him. It is the question that demands explanation. The tempter played his game masterfully.

"Did God *really* say that?" Doubt. That was the starting point of the break between God and humanity. Has God really made such a prohibition? Hearing Eve's response (either embellished or stated more fully) that if the prohibition were violated death would result, the tempter presented his challenge: "You will not certainly die." And finally came the bait: "For God knows that when you eat from it your eyes will be opened, and you will be like God, knowing good and evil." (See Genesis 3:1–5.)

Once it was acknowledged that God did say something, then came the counter perspective. This was in fact a challenge to take on God. "Surely you will not die if you disobey what He said. In fact, you will have the same power as God." The same three temptations were used in the wilderness with Jesus, except that fully understanding with whom he was dealing, the tempter camouflaged the temptations (see Matthew 4:1–11). But the progression from doubting God's promise to autonomy and, finally, to the offer of one's own kingdom apart from God's purposes is the same pattern of seduction. The tempter's formula never changes, just the entry point.

If the Genesis account of the first temptation is studied, there are three panels to it. The first is to doubt that God has spoken. The second is to challenge God with impunity. The third is to indict God's reasoning: Has God threatened dire consequences of your disobedience to keep you from having the same power that He has? Is it to keep God from having an equal that He has given you these strictures? It is amazing that these temptations to question God's character came before the first humans at a time when they were in perfect fellowship with Him and knew the beauty of His presence and of His gifts in creation and love. But the gift God had given them of the freedom to choose became the abuse of trust.

These temptations are relived every day of our lives. Did God *really* say such and such? The tempter cleverly appealed to the first humans that the reason they should eat the fruit and violate God's law was that they could then play God and set the rules. They could become the God of God, is the implication. How autonomy and power have seduced us across time! But lost in the process was God's presence with them and their perfect relationship with Him. That is at the heart of the story.

It is important to understand that God's purpose for us was always perfect fellowship with Him. Just as water is to the body the presence of God is to the soul. In freely choosing to violate His law, we forfeited the consummate fulfillment of our spiritual longing.

Presence, relationship, holiness, trust, beauty, goodness, peace—all were present in the relationship between God and humanity at creation. By playing God and redefining good and evil according to our own discretion, we introduced into the human spirit disobedience, absence, severance, distrust, evil, and restlessness.

It is the most telling reality that by eating of the tree of the knowledge of good and evil, we uprooted that tree and today, in the day of environmental protection, all trees are protected except that one. We want to hold God accountable to our notion of good, but we want to do away with the notion of evil and be accountable to nobody. We use our freedom to try to free ourselves from the very One who gives us our freedom. We want the gift without the giver. The symptom of evil remains—suffering—but we expunge the cause of evil—our own responsibility.

By changing the metanarrative of God's story, we have sought to change the narrative in our own lives and the result is, in

one word: *brokenness.* We may call it independence or autonomy or coming of age or postmodern or progressive or political
correctness. But in reality it is that we are broken. Renaming
something doesn't change its essence. Our bluff will be called.
Let me say it again: What has happened is that we have been
broken. Life is broken. We are broken and splintered individuals. We have enslaved ourselves in violation of the purpose for
which we were created, and the result has been a shattering of
everything we were intended to be. The Bible calls it sin. And
pain is that constant reminder of our brokenness.

Søren Kierkegaard, the Danish philosopher, said,

> If I had in my service a submissive Jinni who, when I
> asked for a glass of water, would bring me the world's
> most expensive wines, deliciously blended in a goblet, I
> would dismiss him until he learned that the enjoyment
> consists not in what I enjoy but in getting my own way.[6]

"Getting my own way." We simply do not like the word *sin*
and would rather call it anything else.

Let's look at sin with a different lens. What is sin? Ultimately, it is redefining God's intended purpose for your life
and charting your own course. When God says the body is
sacred according to the definition that He has given, sin is
redefining His purpose and desacralizing the body. When He
gives us laws by which to live, sin is rebelling against God's
rules and making our own rules. When He defines love, sin
is profaning it for use to our own ends, as we define them.
When He tells us there are consequences to disobedience, sin
is demanding leniency when we flagrantly and unrepentantly

break His laws. When God offers grace and forgiveness and love when we have fallen short, sin is spurning Him for ourselves while demanding a higher standard of laws for others.

Sin is changing the purpose of God for our lives and becoming self-serving. This pertains to all matters with which we are entrusted. Whether time, money, words, commitments, relationships, or stewardship, we are given the freedom and responsibility to honor those particulars in a manner that is consistent with our God-given purpose. God's Word given to humanity has been redefined by humanity. His Word was specific, but we have scrambled it up, thinking we know better.

An illustration of what I am saying comes from our language. The word *therapist* signifies one who is trained to help a person feel well, whether a psychotherapist or a physiotherapist. Therapy is the process employed to make the person well. If you break the word *therapist* in two a certain way, you no longer have a therapist, you have "the rapist." One makes you well; the other plunders you. A simple rearrangement has huge ramifications.

Another example can be found in a paraphrasing of Paul's injunction in Ephesians 4:28: "Let him that stole, steal no more. Let him labor with his hands." If the punctuation is changed just slightly, you have "Let him that stole, steal. No more let him labor with his hands."

I recently saw a T-shirt that read:

Come and eat, Grandma
Come and eat Grandma

Commas Make a Difference

Truth is primarily a property of propositions, and when you rearrange them or toy with the words or change the meaning, you redefine reality. This was the malady of free choices at the dawn of human existence. "Did God *really* say...?"

Where Is the Wound?

What happens when a person is stabbed to death? The physical system first reacts in pain to the destruction and then is silenced because of the total severance of the body from life support—death. It is the same with the soul. Sin is the stabbing to death of the spirit, causing a severance between spiritual life and the spiritual capacity of the person. The person is then no longer the carrier of the body, but the body carries the person. The shell walks and moves, but the being is dead.

That was not the way God intended us to be, and that is why it has been said that "the worst effect of sin is within, and is manifest not in poverty, and pain, and bodily defacement, but in the discrowned faculties, the unworthy love, the low ideal, and the brutalized and enslaved spirit."[7]

Sin is the cause. A disconnection from the spirit is the result. Pain is the symptom. The worst judgment upon sin is more sin. Bereft of the presence of God, the isolation is rightly called death. Fyodor Dostoevsky said that hell is the inability to love.[8] I can take it one step further: Hell is the self, isolated from God. His Word has been violated, His presence has been lost, and the pain we feel is that of being alone.

Many years ago I underwent major back surgery. An incident from that surgery gives me nightmares to this very day. As the initial medication wore off, the first hint of pain and the growing sense of a burning sensation told me I had gone under the blade. The huge padding and dressing was still fresh and provided support for the fresh stitches. For two days I was motionless.

When I experienced the first desire to turn on my side for just a few moments, it took two nurses to skillfully use a sheet to hold my weight and gently turn me over. It was done so gently, gradually, and methodically, with skill and purpose. They told me to ring for them when I needed to shift positions again. The next time I needed to move, they used the same routine.

At about the midnight hour I asked for the night duty nurse to get the assistance of another and to help me onto my side once again. She left to find help but came back saying that everyone else was busy with other patients so she would manage on her own. I pleaded with her to wait until someone else was free because the wound was still fresh and throbbing, but she assured me that she was strong enough, skilled enough, and experienced enough to manage it on her own.

Before I could make a second plea, she dug her hands underneath my mid-back to flip me over and, almost blacking out, I screamed in agony while tears flowed uncontrollably. I lay there clutching the sheet, wishing for somebody to help me...anyone but her. She immediately pulled back her hands in dismay, looked at them, and said, "Oh my goodness! You've had *back* surgery? I thought it was a hip replacement and that's why I tried to turn you over this way!"

I shall refrain from giving my thoughts regarding such incredible ignorance. That happened more than ten years ago, and I still shudder at the memory. The next day when I told the surgeon what had happened, he did not spare *his* thoughts. Some days later I had to be taken back into surgery to have the incision re-stitched. Whether this incident had anything to do with it, I do not know. But I do know that I had never felt such searing, ravaging pain in my life. It was like a knife running down my spine and twisting in there.

You see, sin is the brokenness of the soul, a wound that is deep and systemic, and pain is the symptom. Handling it inappropriately increases the agony, and a misdiagnosis only mangles the wound and results in more pain. In the hands of a skilled nurse, I could cope with the pain. The ministrations of one who didn't even know why I was there and tore at the wound—even inadvertently—were torture.

There is a purpose to life, and sin is the violation of that purpose. The starting point of dealing with pain is to understand and accept that there is a purpose to your life and to mine. We are not just thrust into existence indiscriminately; rather, we are here by the divine will of our Creator God. What is life's purpose? The Bible makes it clear that the ultimate purpose of God for us is communion with the Father. Not union, not just submission or being absorbed into His being, but *communion* with Him, friend to friend.

Let me illustrate what this means. I am now a grandfather. No great accomplishment on my part, just a reality. One day my daughter, watching me enjoy my little grandson, asked me, "What's the difference between having a child and a grandchild?" I paused to think about her question, and then I said, "When you are a parent, you hold and raise that little one with an incredible expenditure of energy, work, expense, sleeplessness, worry. All that extracts from you a major portion of the limited stock of emotional and physical energy each of us has been given. But when you're a grandparent, a greater portion of your stock of energy can now be used in the enjoyment and delight a child brings because its parents are there to give the direct care. The love you feel may be the same, but while the parents feel the strain and responsibility of loving the child, the grandparents are free to *enjoy* loving the child."

But let me switch to the child now. The child comes as a total stranger into the world. The look of bewilderment is evident from the beginning. The very first experience of the child as it enters the world is pain. Isn't it odd that the first sound is not laughter but crying? How incredible it would be if a baby were delivered laughing. But the reality isn't so. The first smile comes only after months, after the child has grown accustomed to the familiar and recognizes what care and provision mean. Only then comes the smile, the giggle, the chuckle, and the longing to be with those who personify love to that child.

The little one knows what communion with its earthly parents means. Is that not an indicator of what life was meant to be in our relationship with our heavenly parent? The little one does not have to be taught to cry. Laughter comes with the familiarity of love. Pain comes from unfamiliarity, estrangement, puzzlement, aloneness, and physical and emotional isolation. The baby learns to smile in response to being cradled, comforted, held, protected, and loved. When Augustine said, "You have made us for yourself, and our hearts are restless until they find their rest in thee,"[9] this is precisely what he was talking about.

God has a general purpose for life and a specific purpose for each of us in knowing His presence in our souls. He communes with us there. The physical is indicative of the spiritual. The naturalist experiences great loss by limiting himself to matter and denying the world beyond it. The great loss of the pantheist is in attempting to ignore the body, the material, and see only the soul.

Why are so many songs that are written preoccupied with love? Why is there always a "broken heart," when we actually mean that our emotions are torn? Is it because we are searching for the touch to the soul that comes only from knowing the reason for our being? No matter how the naturalist focuses on science or the pantheist on detachment from the material, the people of this world cry out for meaning and purpose in their existence.

The Oldest Book with the Oldest Problem

The context of the entire book of Job—the book in the Bible that deals most with this subject—is pain. "Why?" Job asked from various vantage points, but not once did he question God's existence. He struggled with wanting to know God's purpose and understand His ways. Job wondered about the purpose of his own existence, but he never questioned God's existence. Deep within he ultimately recognized that outside of God there were no answers, just haunting questions. But in the philosophical and the theological pursuits of the answers to the reality of his experience two realities emerged, one negative and the other positive.

First, the negative: the colossal failure of his friends. They were at their best when they took time out of their own lives just to be with him, saying nothing. The moment they began to give their own observations for why Job was suffering and offer their suggestions for remedying his situation, Job's pain intensified. To be loved and feel cared about is what someone who is hurting needs from friends. The person who is experiencing pain and suffering simply needs to know that he or she is not alone. Let me give you an example of this.

A dear friend of mine passed away recently. In his final few days, he was in agony. In my last visit with him, I took his hand and prayed with him as I was preparing to leave while his wife and daughter stood nearby. I thanked God for a faithful wife and family. How the children loved their father! How this wife loved her husband! Even though he was in such indescribable physical pain, it was not his pain but the mention of his family in my prayer that brought his tears. The soul longs for the balm that touches the soul beyond the body, the balm that comes from being in the presence of those beloved ones. Job's friends increased his hurt by judging him rather than just being near him and comforting him with their presence.

Fifty years after leading me to Christ when I was seventeen, the man who brought the Bible to me in my hospital room after my attempted suicide lay dying himself, miles away from me. When I called him on the telephone, he told me how much pain he was suffering. His whole body was racked in pain, his body breaking down from the mismanagement of diabetes. My heart went out to him.

He spoke in the fondest terms of our friendship. Even in his pain, his daughter told me he would ask her to access YouTube clips of me so he could watch them. On one occasion he asked his son-in-law, "Could you please just hold me for a while?"

His daughter said that a blind woman from their church came every day of her own volition to give him a foot massage, and her dad would cry through it with unspeakable gratitude as his dried, calloused feet were held in the hands of a sensitive heart. That caring touch spoke volumes to his soul.

Each time I think of that, I tear up. Are we not hearing the cries of those who just want to be held, to be touched, to know that they are not alone? Those who have turned into recluses and who die alone have already died within long before their physical bodies give up. Starved of relationships for so long, they no longer know how to relate, and the desire of many is for distance rather than closeness.

In fact, some time ago one of the world's wealthiest women separated herself from her family. The owner of a forty-five-room mansion in New York filled with artwork worth millions of dollars, she spent the last few years of her life in a rented hospital room just to be separated from the opulence and the family that was embroiled in a bitter struggle for ownership. Among her last words were these: "Money is poison." What she had in plenty was in disproportion to what she needed the most. The soul was left empty, displaced by matter, and her aloneness was expressing that desolation. The care of a friend is often the first touch to reawakening the soul.

So the failure we see in the story of Job is the failure of friendship. Then comes the answer of God. God's answer was not propositional, but relational. And that is what Job most needed. He simply needed to know that God was with him through his ordeal . . . that God had not abandoned him.

Pain can easily produce the sense of being abandoned. The presence of someone who loves and cares can most persuasively counter that fear. God's words were important to Job, but most important to him was the assurance that God was with him through it all, revealing Himself to Job at the most critical moment. And Job said, "My ears had heard of you but now my eyes have seen you" (Job 42:5).

Calvin Miller sums it up well when he speaks of answers that come in the form of words and other answers that come in the form of God's presence:

> The sermon and the Spirit always work in combination to produce liberation. Sometimes the Spirit and sermon do supply direct answers to human need, but most often they answer indirectly. Most problems are not solved by listening to sermons. The sermon, no matter how sincere, cannot solve these unsolvable problems. So if the sermon is not a problem solver, where shall we go for solutions? Together with the Spirit, the sermon exists to point out that having answers is not essential to living. What is essential is the sense of God's presence during dark seasons of questioning... Our need for specific answers is dissolved in the greater issue of the Lordship of Christ over all questions— those that have answers and those that don't.[10]

To some questions there are answers; to other questions there are no sufficient propositional answers. Both dissolve in the reality of God's presence, and the answers we do have about Him carry us through the questions for which we still don't have the answers. God has made us for that special relationship with Him. That is the purpose of life, that we might know God and enjoy His presence in our souls.

In their hostile, hate-multiplying world, it is not by accident that the crass materialists who are represented by the new atheists mock the greatest witness within their own souls as the most worthy of ridicule: The presence of God, who is most needed by them, is seen as the least worthy of all arguments and the most worthy of contempt.

A baby's initial smile as it recognizes love ought to give us the first clue of who has ultimately created us. God's presence brings a smile to the soul.

Where Is the Hope?

So now we arrive at the next step.

We have an author.

We have a story.

We have a purpose.

We have the breakdown of that purpose.

We have the answer of God's presence.

We come now to the most unique perspective on the road to recovery. It is not morality that gets us back. Morality will always be dependent on our laws and our wills, and both are totally at the mercy of an individual and the society in which he lives. The answer lies in the very process of God entering into that suffering and providing the gift of grace to us for forgiveness and inner strength. Vince will expand on this.

So here we have it. Our greatest gift from God is freedom. Our greatest blessing is His presence—perfect love and relationship. On this basis I move to two converging conclusions.

First, the real malady is *within* us. The brokenness is *in* you and me. And because of that there are two ways God can enable us to cope with suffering: He can completely remove the pain by answering our prayers every time we ask Him to remove an obstacle. But think about that. Today perhaps it is a broken arm. Tomorrow it may be a bankrupt relative. The next day it could be a dying loved one. Problems will forever remain intrinsic to the human scene. Do we play God and demand that the evil be removed at every occurrence? That is asking for the logically impossible if love is to be supreme; God doesn't want us to love Him for what we can get from Him.

The other way God enables us to cope with suffering is to change us from within. He changes our hearts and walks with us through the deep waters. This is the greater miracle when compared to the mere changing of circumstances. Only a change within us can keep intact Paul's three excellencies of faith, hope, and love.

Second, the pattern of the story makes sense. The narrative goes from the fact of our brokenness to a Savior who entered into our suffering and brought us the hope of His eternal presence. This is how I see the story summarized:

Where there is the possibility of love, there has to be the reality of freedom.

Where there is the reality of freedom, there has to be the possibility of pain.

Where there is the reality of pain, there is the need for a Savior.

Where there is a Savior, there is the possibility of redemption.

From the freedom to love, to the possibility of suffering, to the provision of a Savior, to the message of redemption, to our restoration: That is the story of the gospel of Jesus Christ and His redemption provided for you and for me.

This second conclusion suggests that pain holds a legitimate place in our lives. You see, the bottom line is this: Our problem is not that we are immoral. Our problem is so severe that it cannot be solved by morality alone. Only the Creator of our souls who gave us our essence can lift us to the plane where we see the Savior's wounds as our redemption.

Is it not possible for God, who has shown us why physical pain is important, to show us in His infinite wisdom how pain serves the ultimate purpose of calling us to our Savior and Redeemer? Malcolm Muggeridge put it in these words:

Contrary to what might be expected, I look back on experiences that at the same time seemed especially desolating and painful with particular satisfaction. Indeed, I can say with complete truthfulness that everything I have learned in my seventy-five years in this world, everything that has enhanced and truly enlightened my existence, has been through affliction and not through happiness, whether pursued or attained. In other words, if it ever were to be possible to eliminate affliction from our earthly existence...the result would not be to make life delectable, but to make it too banal and trivial to be endurable. This, of course, is what the cross signifies. And it is the cross, more than anything else, that has called me inexorably to Christ.[11]

I have thought of Muggeridge's statement often because I so admire his writings. In his younger days, he would have lampooned anyone he heard say the same thing. But after years of learning and writing and seeing and finally trusting Jesus Christ, he saw through a different lens. Satire creates a clever caricature of reality, and as a humorist and satirist, Muggeridge could mock anything. As a testimonial to life's most enduring truths, he went to Christ and to the cross and he was made most real. Nothing trivial there.

It is not accidental that the very word *excruciating* literally means "out of the cross." Nowhere was pain more embodied than on the cross. Nowhere else was the redefinition of life given than from the cross. Jesus Christ continually contradicts us in the way we experience ourselves as alive and shows us how to redefine life.

Not in Spite of but Through

I close this chapter with a very profound statement from James Stewart of Scotland. Psalm 68:18, in the King James translation that Stewart taught from, is translated as "He led captivity captive." Stewart says:

The very triumphs of His foes, it means, He used for their defeat. He compelled their dark achievements to subserve His ends, not theirs. They nailed Him to the tree, not knowing that by that very act they were bringing the world to His feet. They gave Him a cross, not guessing

that He would make it a throne. They flung Him outside
the gates to die, not knowing that in that very moment
they were lifting up all the gates of the universe, to let the
King come in. They thought to root out His doctrines,
not understanding that they were implanting imperish-
ably in the hearts of men the very name they intended
to destroy. They thought they had God with His back to
the wall, pinned and helpless and defeated: they did not
know that it was God Himself who had tracked them
down. He did not conquer *in spite of* the dark mystery of
evil. He conquered *through* it.[12]

Maybe this is what the Chinese pastor in Indonesia meant
when he said that it is necessary to experience pain and suffering if life is to be fully lived and understood. God conquers
through it. Maybe this is what the mother meant when she
prayed that her daughter would be able to feel pain. Maybe
this is what the apostle Paul meant when he said, "That I may
know him, and the power of his resurrection, and the fellowship of his sufferings, being made conformable unto his
death" (Philippians 3:10 KJV).

Love and forgiveness, worth and worship—all are con-
ditional on freedom. It is these that form the components of
growing with Jesus Christ and finding in His presence hope
that transcends the moment and lifts our hearts to the eternal.
If people become skeptics about God in response to suffering,
we must assume that the antidote, pleasure, must mean perpet-
ual happiness. But that is simply not the case. Chesterton suggested that meaninglessness does not come from being weary
of pain. Rather, meaninglessness comes from being weary of

pleasure. In short, both pain and pleasure are experiences that remind us that without God, neither can be explained.

I fully realize that to an aching heart no volume of words can bring comfort. But it is also true that even if the impact is not immediate, at some moment, the truth takes hold.

I believe God best understands why we weep and why we struggle. I recall some years ago being on a flight and, during the descent, a baby was screaming with pain; one could tell that the little one's ears must have been hurting. I could feel the sudden descent triggering discomfort in my own ears. Everyone was intently swallowing, or trying to pop their ears, but the child just kept screaming.

I turned around to see how the mother was handling it. I saw her holding the baby to her chest with her head leaned back, tears running down her face. How could she properly explain to the child that soon they would be at their destination and the pain would cease?

I couldn't help but think of Jesus at the tomb of Lazarus (John 11:1–44). This family at Bethany was very special to Him. He was the friend they needed the most when Lazarus was dying, but He wasn't there. So when Jesus did come, their biggest question was why He hadn't come before Lazarus died. He assured them that He was indeed the One who could and would still rescue Lazarus. "We know you will do that in the final resurrection," they said, "but had you been here, this death could have been prevented." And the Gospel writer tells us that Jesus stood by the grave and wept.

Then, with the authority Jesus alone had, He called Lazarus forth from the grave. The power He had, He displayed. And the sorrow He felt in the face of the death of a friend was not hidden either. Why the tears? Why the heartache? He knew He was going to raise Lazarus from the grave. I suspect like the mother clutching her child, Jesus must have wondered, *How do I explain to them that when they reach their destination, the pain will be gone?*

Tears are part of our stories, but our eternal destination point is hard to explain to us because we know only time and cannot understand eternity. But He will get us there.

CHAPTER 3

—❧—

A RESPONSE OF GRACE

Vince Vitale

Some of my reflections about suffering began with a conversation I had with my aunt Regina many years ago at a family gathering for Christmas. She spoke with me about how difficult it was for her to see her son Charles—my cousin—suffer from a serious mental illness.

Being more concerned at the time with the question than the questioner, I began to tell Aunt Regina some of my more abstract, philosophical explanations for why God might allow evils such as Charles's suffering. But after listening very graciously, Aunt Regina turned to me and said, "But Vince, that doesn't speak to me as a mother."

Explanations were not what my aunt needed at that moment. Sometimes we do need explanations; as a philosopher, I'm fully committed to that. But other times we just need to know that there is someone who understands what we're going through and cries along with us.

Some of you reading this will engage with what I say

primarily from an intellectual perspective. Others of you are presently in the very trenches of suffering. I'm going to do my best to be sensitive to this variety of perspectives, but I want to apologize in advance if anything I say comes across as if I'm not taking seriously any real-life suffering you are dealing with. I genuinely hope that will not be the case.

I also recognize that for some of you, the Church has been guilty of wronging you in some way—of causing you to suffer or of failing to be there for you when you needed it most. The Church is my family. I love it, and I am so grateful to be a part of it, but we make mistakes. Very often we have failed to live up to the love that Jesus calls us to. Before saying any more, I want to apologize on behalf of my family, the Church, and to ask for your forgiveness for any time that we have been the cause of suffering in your life. I hope that will never be the case again, and I hope you will give us another chance to earn your trust.

In one form or another, every one of us has faced the problem of suffering; that is why I focused on it in my graduate studies. It is a challenge I have faced. It is a challenge those whom I love have faced. Grappling with this challenge has brought me frustration and tears. It has also brought me understanding, strength, comfort, and hope—gifts I pray for each one of you as you consider the responses offered in this book.

A Free-Fall Response

The response of freedom that Ravi discussed in the last chapter highlights the culpability of human persons for the suffering of this world. Free choices against God, free choices against one another, choosing hate or indifference toward those we were created to love and defend—this is the root of so much of the brokenness that we find ourselves in and that we find in ourselves.

This is the testimony of the Bible from its very first pages; right from the start Christianity confronts the challenge of suffering head-on.

There is no shortage of debate about how to interpret some of the details of these first few chapters of Genesis, or about how these chapters relate to cosmology and biology. But in broad strokes, what do we find?

We find a story of people who deep in their hearts know God, and who also know what He has asked of them. But then they hear this voice in their ears: "Did God really say, 'You must not eat from any tree in the garden'?" (Genesis 3:1). And, as Ravi explained, they begin to doubt God. They begin to doubt that He knows what's best for them; they begin to doubt that He is *for* them; ultimately, they begin to doubt what He has actually said—His Word.

And then they sin. They do what they know deep down they should not do. Not a big sin, just eating a piece of fruit that they were told not to eat. No big deal, right?

But it starts them down a path. First we're told that they felt shame. They were convinced that God wouldn't want anything to do with them anymore, and so they hid themselves from God. Maybe some of us can relate to that.

Then they began accusing each other. Adam pointed at Eve and said "She did it!" (in essence pointing his finger at God as well by referring to Eve as "the woman *you* put here with me"

[Genesis 3:12, emphasis added]); and Eve pointed at the serpent and said "He did it!"

From temptation to doubt to disobedience to shame to hiding to finger-pointing to suffering.

People sometimes spend much time debating about what the beginning of Genesis says about science. That debate involves important questions. But we must be wary of the tendency to avoid facing what else the text says:

From temptation to doubt to disobedience to shame to hiding to finger-pointing to suffering.

Is there really a question of whether this story speaks the truth about the human heart?

When I read it, I have to admit that it resounds with the truth about me. If we're going to honestly ask the question "Why suffering?" we need to start as G. K. Chesterton supposedly did when a newspaper asked him to respond to the question "What's wrong with the world?":

Dear Sirs,
I am.
Sincerely yours,
G. K. Chesterton.[1]

But here's the most amazing part of the story of the Fall. The first persons have rejected God. They've decided they'd rather be their own gods. And how does God respond?

He goes looking for them; He pursues them; He calls out to them: "Where are you?"

Then, after their first interaction with God after they have sinned, Adam names his wife "Eve." It's a name of great honor. *Eve* is often understood to mean "breath" or "life," and it is given to her "because she would become the mother of all the living" (Genesis 3:20); symbolically, it connects her with God's breathing of life into Adam. And even the spellings of the names Eve and Yahweh show similarities in the original Hebrew.[2] They have the same ending. In English, it would be something like a daughter Hanna having a mother named Joanna.

This is probably not the name Eve expected to be called after helping to cause the Fall of all humanity! But even then, in her moment of great sin, she receives the honor of a name that symbolically connects her with God Himself. Even amid the consequences of the Fall, how generous and loving must God's interaction with them have been for Adam to choose that name for his wife?

And then we're told that God "made garments of skin for Adam and [Eve]" (Genesis 3:21). In ancient Middle Eastern culture, this was the exact opposite of what should have happened. Their clothes should have been torn to symbolize their disgrace.

Instead, God made garments for them. And not only that but the text gives this beautiful detail: "and [He] clothed them" (Genesis 3:21). Imagine the intimacy of God pulling a shirt over your head and carefully guiding your arms through the sleeves, before kneeling down to tie your shoelaces.

God dressed Adam and Eve Himself, so that they would not

be ashamed, foreshadowing that one day He would clothe us in Christ (Galatians 3:27), with the best robe (Luke 15:22), with power from on high (Luke 24:49).

Right from the very beginning, it is in God's response to suffering that we see the love of God most clearly, a love that refuses to give up on us even when we cause great suffering.

A New Response

But someone might *still* press the objection from suffering. One might say, "Even if human persons are responsible for the origin of suffering in the world, it is still God who allows suffering to continue. And how can we possibly trust a God who allows the worst that this world has to offer? What possible purposes could He have, and what possible meaning could He find, in doing so?"

In this chapter I begin to explore a new response to this challenge. I formulated this response in my PhD dissertation after taking cues from a passage written by Gottfried Leibniz in the seventeenth century[3] and from relevant, excellent work published by the philosopher Robert Adams in the 1970s.[4]

This response is consistent with and therefore not in competition with the other responses contained in this book. I offer it not as *the* response, but as one additional angle from which the objection from suffering can be viewed, in the hope that viewing an objection from a variety of angles will help us to see the objection more clearly and thus be better prepared to respond to it. I'd like to share with you the outline of this new approach, and I'd like to do so by telling you a few stories.

First, a true story: My mom and dad met when they were teenagers. They worked in a supermarket—my mom as a cashier and my dad stocking the shelves—and my mom would call for "price checks" when she didn't need them just so she would get to flirt with my dad. (She says he had great shoulders.)

On their first date, they went to a black-tie event in New York City on New Year's Eve, and they fell in love. On their second date, they were standing on the Brooklyn Bridge, overlooking the picturesque New York City skyline, and my dad noticed a ring on my mom's finger.

He asked about it, and she said, "Oh, that's just some ring one of my old boyfriends gave me. I just wear it cause I think it looks nice."

"Oh, yeah, it is nice," my dad responded. "Let me see it."

So my mom took it off and handed it to him, and my dad hurled it off the bridge and watched it sink to the bottom of the East River! "You're with me now," he declared. "You won't be needing that anymore." And my mom loved it! I suspect that was the clinching moment in their relationship.

Well, now that my dad had thrown my mom's ring to the bottom of the East River, it was only fair of him to replace it. So he asked my grandfather for my mom's hand in marriage. As it happens, Grandpa was just about the most intimidating person on the planet. (Just to give you an idea, he once snapped the neck of my brother's pet bird [P.K. the parakeet] with his bare hands because it wouldn't stop chirping while he was trying to take a nap…but that's a story for another day.) Anyway, Grandpa gave the less-than-encouraging response of, "Well Vinnie, we'll cross that bridge when we come to it."

In other words, not anytime soon. "Yes sir, Doctor Palo, yes sir," my dad sputtered.

Long story short, Grandpa wound up in jail, and Dad took that as his opportunity to finally cross that bridge. He asked my mom to marry him, she said "Yes!," they got married, and they enjoyed their young married life.

But then, a number of years later, my mom and dad had the crazy idea to procreate—to have a child. They wanted to love me and give me a good life. They realized that this was a grave decision and a grave responsibility. They realized that in having me they would be risking the possibility of serious suffering in my life. But they hoped against it, and they were determined to love me through such suffering if it did occur.

They thought about buying a new pet bird instead, and they considered the fact that if they had a pet bird, they wouldn't be risking nearly as much suffering (especially with Grandpa not around). Birds aren't able to suffer in some of the worst ways that human persons suffer. But my parents didn't want a bird. They wanted me.

Some hope that before long science will allow us to genetically engineer children, ensuring that they are stronger, smarter, and better looking, and perhaps therefore less prone to suffering. But my parents say that even if this technology had been available to them, they wouldn't have been interested. They didn't want a genetically enhanced super-child. They wanted me.

Even before I was born, my parents chose me and they loved me.

My mom was kind enough to carry me for nine months, but it turned out to be only seven months because I was born very prematurely. There were some complications, and I kept my mom in labor for fifty-four hours (sorry, Mom!). Eventually, when my air got cut off, the doctors had to take me out by an emergency cesarean section, and then they immediately rushed me away for tests to see if I was okay.

By the time my mom got to see me, they had shaved one half of my head for one of the tests. And so my mom was counting my fingers and my toes and trying to make sure I was all right, and then she exclaimed, "This is wonderful. He's perfect!... except that he's half-bald, but I'm sure we can get him some hair implants."

Even though it took a fifty-four-hour labor, and even though she thought I was half-bald, my mom says she was grateful, because she got me. And if my mom were to do it all over again—crazy as it sounds—she says she would choose me again. She was willing to pay a great price for me because she couldn't have gotten me otherwise.

What It Takes to Be You

I admit I'm a bit partial to this story, but I do think it is a beautiful tale of love. And I want to suggest that this story of *pro*creation is importantly similar to the story of *God's* creation of the world we live in. I believe one of the reasons that God created and sustains this world, despite its suffering, is because He wants to love you, and me, and all of the people who will ever live.[5]

You might immediately object. You might say, Even if God's intention was to love *us*, surely He should have created *us* in a world with less suffering. This is how we usually frame the problem. We picture ourselves in this world of suffering; then we picture ourselves in a world with far less suffering; and we wonder, *Shouldn't God have created us in the world with far less suffering?* That's a reasonable thought.

However, it's a thought that relies on a philosophical mistake. It relies on the assumption that it would still be *you* and *me* who would exist in that supposedly better world. And I think that assumption is false. Let me explain why.

It was a pretty risky move my dad made when he hurled my mom's ring off the Brooklyn Bridge. Gutsy, no doubt, but risky. Mom loved it! But what if she hadn't? What if she had concluded that my dad had lost it and then run off with her old boyfriend instead? What would that have meant *for me*?

(If you can believe it, fifty years on, my dad is still trying to get my mom to reveal who gave her that ring. Mom flatly refuses to say. Dad suspects it was John Napolitano. John, if you're reading this, remain in hiding.)

I might be tempted to think that if Mom had wound up with her old boyfriend, I could have been better off. I might have been taller. I might have been better looking. Maybe the other guy was royalty. That would have been cool! I could've lived in a castle!

But actually, that's not right. There's a problem with wishing my mom wound up with the other guy, and the problem is this: "I" never would have existed. Maybe some other child would have existed. And maybe he would have been taller and better looking and lived in a castle. But *part* of what makes me who I am—the individual that I am—is my beginning: the parents I have, the sperm and egg I came from, the combination of genes that's true of me. I'm sure my mom and her old boyfriend would have had some very lovely kids, but "I" would not have been one of them.[6]

A similar confusion is at work when we say things like "I was born at the wrong time." Whenever my wife, Jo, forces me to watch Jane Austen films with her, she complains that she was born two hundred years too late because she adores the dresses from back then. What we tend to miss when we reason this way is that it is highly controversial whether we could have existed as the very same persons that we are now in the Georgian Era. A different period of history means different parents, different times of conception, different combinations of genes, all of which result in different people coming to exist.

If we think it through, saying, "I wish my mom had married the other guy," or "I wish I had been born in the Georgian Era," is similar to asking, "Why didn't God create me in a world with far less suffering?" If something as trivial as the throwing of a ring into the East River can alter who comes to be, imagine how radically the history of procreation would be altered if God miraculously removed our propensity to moral evil, or if He miraculously removed our vulnerability to natural disasters and the suffering that they cause. If flipping a ring off a bridge can have a drastic effect on who comes to exist, imagine how radically procreation history would be affected by even *slight* changes in the workings of our natural world, let alone the major changes that would be required to eliminate all suffering. If weather systems or plate tectonics didn't behave as they do, if gravitational and electromagnetic forces had different strengths, if the laws of thermodynamics had undergone a redesign, what would be the results? One plausible result is that none of *us* would have lived.

And still more controversial than whether you could have been born into a world with far less suffering is whether your life in that other world—*even if you could have been born into it*—is a life that it makes sense for you to wish for instead of your current life.

Many have believed throughout history that a human person is, most fundamentally, an immaterial soul. In that case, perhaps your physical origins are not necessary for your identity. Then maybe *technically* God could have created "you"—your immaterial soul—in the Georgian Era or in a suffering-free world.

But even so, would you be "you" in the most important sense? Would it make sense for you to wish for that life rather than your current life even though your hopes, aspirations, projects, loves, relationships, memories, psychology, and biology would all be radically different, even though not a single day you would experience in that life would be much like any day you have actually experienced? Regardless of whether this better-situated person would technically be you, wishing for that life instead of your current life seems worryingly similar to wishing yourself out of existence.

In sum, had the possibilities for suffering in this world been very different, events would have unfolded so differently that an entirely different community of people would have come to exist. Our parents never would have gotten together. They never would have conceived at the precise time that they did.

And therefore "we," as the individuals we are, never would have lived. We often wish we could take some piece of suffering out of the world while keeping everything else the same. But it doesn't work that way. Changing anything changes everything, and everyone.

A Response of Grace

So here's a theological hypothesis: Why is suffering allowed to continue in our world? Perhaps *in part* because God desired to create a specific community of individuals, and allowing suffering made it possible for Him to get precisely the community He desired—a community including you, and me, and every person you see walking down the street.

In one sense this is a new response to the problem of suffering. But its starting points are very old. What I've done is basically theological reflection on a biblical theme. I've tried to take seriously the biblical idea that God had people in mind even before they came to exist:

> Jeremiah 1:4–5: "The word of the Lord came to me, saying, 'Before I formed you in the womb I knew you, before you were born I set you apart.'"

> Ephesians 1:4–5: "[God] chose us in Christ before the foundation of the world to be holy and blameless before him in love. He destined us for adoption as his children through Jesus Christ" (NRSV).

Each of these verses raises a number of theological questions, and explaining the verses thoroughly in their biblical context could take a full chapter or more. But for now I just want to note that there is a general theme in Scripture about God having certain people in mind even before they came to exist. Some verses refer to God's choice of specific people for specific purposes. But since God has control over all that comes to be, there is also a sense in which each and every person is chosen by God—known by Him before conception, knitted together by Him in the womb (Psalm 139:13), loved by Him from all time.

Why didn't God create a world with no possibility of suffering? Why didn't God give up on this world when it fell into great suffering and create one with less suffering instead?[7] Well, He could have, but a loving person is not always drawn to being in relationship with those who suffer least.

I'm reminded of another of my favorite stories, which is about when the parents of one of my best friends first met. At the time, my friend James's mom had just gone through a very difficult divorce and was seven months pregnant. A friend of hers had a convertible and suggested a road trip to get her mind off things. Days later, after little sleep, wearing no makeup and with her auburn hair blown every which way, bordering on both childbirth and an emotional breakdown, James's mom stumbled into James's dad for the first time. After no more than a few sentences had been exchanged between them, James's dad asked her out for coffee, and one coffee turned into two, and two turned into a lifetime.[8]

A few years ago, James asked his dad, "What in the world

were you thinking? Mom must have looked a wreck!" To which the reply came,

"Well, son, I wasn't looking for someone perfect. I was looking for someone I could love."

Maybe God wasn't interested in only perfect people. Maybe He wasn't looking for the most impressive creatures He possibly could have created. Maybe He was just looking for someone He could love. And maybe, like James's dad, He just found Himself—amazingly and against the odds!—with an overwhelming love for us.[9]

Not because we deserved His love. Not because we are better or more impressive or more useful or funnier or better looking than the other people God could have created. Simply out of *grace*—*unmerited* love: the love of a parent standing over his newborn child—not with a grade book, not with an evaluation sheet, not calculating how productive you'll be for the family business, not comparing you to anyone else's kids. Just admiring you, just delighting in you, simply because you are His child. Simply because you are created "in his own image" (Genesis 1:27).

We tend to think we're worthy of love only to the extent that we've been impressive, successful, or beautiful. What a nightmare—always afraid that we'll do something that will make us undeserving of love, or that someone else will come along more deserving of the person we love.

At one point early on in our dating relationship, my now-wife, Jo, turned to me and said, "I don't deserve you." (Between you and me, I think she was fishing for a few compliments.) And you should have seen the look on her face when

I promptly responded, "No, you don't!" But then I continued, "And I don't deserve you either. Isn't it wonderful?"

Pause and consider this question:

What does God think of you? Or, if you're not sure that God exists, what *would* God think of you?

I wonder what the first answer that popped into your mind was. What was the instinctual reaction of your heart?

If you think you need to deserve God's love, then the response to the problem of suffering that I am developing in this chapter will make no sense to you. But Christianity says otherwise. Christianity says that divine love—the best form of love—is not about deserving; it's not about what we earn or merit or accomplish.

God's love is simply about being His child. And therefore, with God you can stop competing to be loved and just enjoy it. The question "Why do you love your child?" doesn't even make sense to a loving parent standing over a newborn infant. "What do you mean, *why* do I love her? She's my child! I made her. She has my nose."

I wonder how much of our suffering results from wishing we were someone else—with someone else's parents, genes, body, face, life? God never wishes you were anyone else. Sure, God could have given up on this world and created something else, but then He wouldn't have gotten you, and He wanted to love you. You were not an accident. God knew you in full—every imperfection, every failure, everything you would ever do wrong—and yet, even before you were born, He chose to give you life.

My cousin Charles, Aunt Regina's son whom I introduced earlier, is an amazing man. The love and kindness with which he has always greeted me is unparalleled. The way he has genuinely rejoiced with me about my life, even when his disability means that his is often a frustration, is one of the most beautiful gifts I have ever received. I have known Charles my whole life, and I have never seen him be unkind to anyone. Not once.

Some would say it would have been better if Charles never existed. There would be less suffering overall. The world would be better off.

I disagree.

Charles's body may be ill, but when I look at him, that's not what I see. I see a man who is exceptional in so many ways. Like my aunt Regina, it's because I know Charles intimately that his suffering is so frustrating. But it's also because I know Charles intimately that I can understand why God loves him so much, and why God would place great value on being able to give Charles life and to pursue life together with him.

For God chose *Charles*—and loved *him*—before the foundation of the world.

Divine Creation and Procreation

I mentioned earlier that this chapter's response to the problem of suffering is different from—though fully consistent with—the claim that much suffering is due to free human choices. The response of this chapter is also not to be confused with a soul-making approach,[10] according to which God allows suffering because it is through dealing with suffering that we form our characters and live more meaningful lives overall. No doubt there is value in this soul-making approach; suffering does often lead to character formation and to an appreciation of what is truly meaningful in life. But the approach of this chapter highlights something different: not that through suffering you will live a better or more meaningful life than the life you would have lived without suffering, but rather that without suffering you never would have existed in the first place.

This suggests that the possibilities for a Christian response to the problem of suffering are richer and more numerous than typically assumed. The explanation for suffering is to be found not only in past human guilt or future human potential, but also in each person's status as a present and enduring object of God's love.

This response of grace to the challenge of suffering finds a strong analogy in human procreation, where parents act not to make an existing child's life better but rather to give life itself.

I joked earlier about having a child being a crazy idea, but the truth is, it is a much more sobering decision than we tend to appreciate. Note that in normal cases of procreation, parents risk bringing a child into a lot of suffering; even the most fortunate of human lives is accompanied by seasons of serious suffering. Even more than that, parents procreate knowing full well that one day the child will suffer death.

We don't usually think of things this way, and rightfully so. We want to focus on the positive and hopeful aspects of having a child rather than the negative ones. But the truth remains that by having a child, parents are doing something that they know will result in the child they procreate suffering death.

Now, typically it is very hard to justify doing something

that you know will lead to another human person suffering severely and dying. Why, then, do we think that having a child is morally permissible, and can even be loving and courageous? Because the child who comes to exist would not have existed otherwise. In bringing a child into the world, we risk great suffering, but in doing so we bestow on someone not just any good, but the good of life itself. What I have been suggesting is that, similarly, in creating and sustaining this world rather than some other world, God bestowed on each of us not just any good, but the good of life.

If someone thinks it would be in principle immoral to create someone in a world that includes the likelihood of serious suffering, she will not only need to call God evil, she will also need to call evil anyone who decides to have a child. What follows is that if there is good reason to think that human procreation can be an act of love—despite its great cost—then there is also good reason to think that God's creation of the world we live in could be an act of love.

And, in fact, God is in an even better moral position than human parents, with respect to both the beginning and the end of human life. Whereas human parents can only aim in procreation for a human person generally (and then wait to see who they get), God can be understood as aiming for specific individuals. And whereas human parents are often helpless to defeat suffering in the lives of their children, God has the power to offer each created person the ultimate defeat of suffering in a heavenly and eternal home with Him. The weight of suffering is sometimes so great that it causes us to doubt the goodness of life; only God can ultimately lift that weight and put our doubts to rest.

Three Clarifications

Three clarifications are worth noting at this point.

First, that we would not have come to exist in a world without suffering does not entail that God *created* or *caused* evil and suffering in order to bring us into existence. It only implies that one reason God might *allow* evil and suffering to continue once it entered the world is out of a desire to love the individuals who would come to exist.

One might push back here, saying that even if God only *allows* suffering resulting from moral evil, surely He directly *causes* natural suffering such as earthquakes and tornadoes. Not necessarily. The philosopher Peter van Inwagen, for instance, notes that earthquakes and tornadoes are not intrinsically evil. They are evil only when people are in the wrong place at the wrong time. Van Inwagen suggests that at some point in the earth's history, God raised beings to a state of rationality and moral awareness and then brought them into intimate relationship with Himself. In that state of untainted union with God, van Inwagen wonders whether these first human persons would have had a sort of sixth sense that always allowed them to not be in the wrong place at the wrong time. The loss of this sense when these persons fell into estrangement from God, van Inwagen theorizes, would be just as natural a consequence as the loss of human language is for a feral child.[11] Thus, there are coherent theories according to which even so-called natural suffering can be traced back to free decisions against God, and therefore understood as allowed by God rather than directly caused by Him.

Relatedly, the fact that God knows the details of the future does not mean that He directly *causes* future evil and suffering. There are a variety of ways to show this, one of which I am reminded of every time I find myself knowing before she acts that my three-year-old goddaughter is about to do something mischievous. I know she is about to do this not because I *cause* her to do it, but because I know her very well. Even more so should it be unsurprising if the God who knows the number of hairs on our heads (Matthew 10:30; Luke 12:7) is able to know how the future will unfold without being to blame for all of its badness.[12]

Second, that we would not have existed without suffering does not mean that we cannot one day exist in a suffering-free heavenly state. If you change the details of my origin, my mom doesn't have me with my dad but winds up having some other kid with her old boyfriend. But, once I exist, you can change the details of my life greatly without threatening my existence. For example, in the future I might live in America or in the United Kingdom. Either way, it will be *me* who lives there. And in the same way, one day each of us can live in an eternal and suffering-free kingdom while remaining fully ourselves.

Third, nothing that I have said implies that God does not regret suffering, or that choosing to allow suffering is an easy choice for Him. I suspect it is no easier than the choice to bring a child into this world. It is a sobering decision, and a decision mixed with great regret at the suffering that will accompany the creation of life. But, nevertheless, I believe it is a decision made out of love—love proved by the readiness of the Creator to suffer alongside those He creates and to see them through that suffering at any and all costs. In chapter 4 ("A Response at the Cross") and chapter 7 ("A Response of Hope"), I will suggest that God has proved His love in just these ways.

Reframing the Question

Is this meant to be an exhaustive response answering every aspect of the problem of suffering? No. But when considered alongside the variety of responses given in this book, I think it helps to show that the objection from suffering is more complicated than it might first appear.

What kind of world we think God would create and sustain depends on what we think God would value. What if one of the things God values—values greatly and unconditionally— is you?

What if He valued a world in which you would exist, and in which your parents would exist, and your grandparents, and your ancestors before them? Suppose He wanted them. Suppose He wanted a world in which every generation in every part of the world is made up of people He has chosen, because He loves them and desires to call them into relationship with Himself.

We think we wish God had allowed a different sort of world to exist, but in doing so we unwittingly wish ourselves, and those we love, out of existence. And so the problem of suffering is reframed in the form of a question: Could God have wronged you by creating a world in which you came to exist and are offered eternal life, rather than creating a different world in which you never would have lived?[13]

CHAPTER 4

---*&*---

A RESPONSE AT THE CROSS

Vince Vitale

Returning to my parents' story, it's important to note that when choosing whether to have me, it wasn't just potential suffering in *my* life that my parents had to consider; they also had to consider what it would cost *them* to have me and to raise me.

Love requires sacrifice. It requires a willingness to suffer alongside those you love. So my mom gave birth to me, and then she sacrificed countless hours of sleep to care for me. In fact, when I was an infant, I wouldn't go to sleep unless I was holding my mom's hand. And so, rather than let me cry myself to sleep, my mom pulled a mattress into my room and slept night after night with her hand uncomfortably stretched up into my crib, holding my hand.

Eventually we got past that stage, but then one day, when I was about six, I was out playing football on my next-door neighbor's front lawn with a bunch of older kids, and I was getting knocked around pretty good.

And I came running home crying to my mom, who was out on the front porch, yelling in protest, "I'm not tough enough! I'm not tough enough!"

So guess what my mom did?

She did what any loving mother of a six-year-old son would do. She lowered herself into an athletic stance, with her hands resting on her bent knees. And then she hung her nose out in the air, looked at me lovingly, and said "Punch me in the nose! Punch me in the nose! Come on! You are tough enough! Punch me in the nose!"

At first I just looked at her like she was crazy, and indeed she was, but she persisted: "Punch me in the nose! Punch me in the nose!"

Well, she asked for it. I don't know what sort of psychological state I must have been in, but finally, I reared back and gave my mom a straight right hand to the nose. And, to my astonishment, blood began pouring out of her nose and down her face.

But then came one of the most gorgeous images I have ever seen. Through the blood came the most dazzling, radiant, joyful smile, and my mom said, "Now get back out there!"

Christians worship a God who, like my mom, was willing to come and suffer alongside us—a God who would not remain comfortably seated on some far-off heavenly throne as we suffered. He could not bear to. As a caring parent, He came alongside His children in the person of Jesus Christ, and He suffered with us.

"Jesus wept" (John 11:35) at the tomb of His friend Lazarus; even when we can muster no words to express it, He knows the grief of losing a loved one. And His experience of suffering did not stop there. The night before Jesus died, as He wrestled with what He knew the next day would bring, He said to His friends, "My soul is overwhelmed with sorrow to the point of death" (Matthew 26:38). Imagine the God of the universe—the Creator of all things—saying He is overwhelmed with sorrow, even to death.

If you've ever experienced deep depression or thought about dying, Jesus is right there with you. There is no depth of agony and helplessness we can experience in this life that He doesn't understand.

The loving parent is not the one who never allows suffering in a child's life. The loving parent is the one who is willing to suffer alongside his children. In creating this world, God didn't merely *accept* the cost, but He *suffered* the cost.

In the height of irony, it may be the famous atheist and philosopher Friedrich Nietzsche who said it best. He wrote,

> The gods justified human life by living it themselves—the only satisfactory [response to the problem of suffering] ever invented.[1]

Remarkably, Nietzsche was writing of the ancient Greeks here and, in his bias, didn't make the connection to Christianity! But as a Christian, I am very pleased to agree with him and then point emphatically to the cross of Jesus Christ.

At the cross, we see the absolute uniqueness of the Christian response to suffering. In Islam, the idea of God suffering is nonsense; it is thought to make God weak. For many Buddhists, to reach divinity is precisely to move beyond the possibility of suffering, to give up your attachments to other people so that you will never have to suffer for anyone. Only in Christ do we have a God who loves us enough to suffer with us.

Goodness Explained vs. Goodness Displayed

These thoughts highlight a key distinction between goodness *explained* and goodness *displayed*. There are two ways to defend the goodness of a person when he or she is accused of wrongdoing. The first way is to explain the good reasons the person had for acting as he or she did. This is the more traditional approach to responding to the problem of evil, to respond by telling a story about *why* God might create and sustain a world that turned out like this one. This method seeks to unveil (at least some of) the *reasons* God has for allowing evil and suffering. I took this approach in chapter 3. I suggested that *one* reason why God allows suffering is so that He can create and love a specific community of persons—a community that includes you and me.

But there is also a second way to defend the goodness of God against objections from suffering, and this second way is just as rational. Let me try to illustrate it.

My mom did eventually get up from my knockdown blow, and the Vitales lived together as a family for several years without too much significant suffering. But then, about ten years ago, my dad felt a sharp pain in his leg and had to be rushed to the hospital.

Dr. Frasco—a topflight vascular surgeon—found my family in the hospital waiting room and told us that he needed to operate, and that although there wasn't time to explain why due to the complexity of my dad's condition, there was a good chance he would have to amputate my dad's leg.

Despite Dr. Frasco's qualifications, it was tempting in this situation to question him, to be suspicious of his prognosis and his chosen course of action. My dad looked perfectly healthy from the outside. Maybe this surgeon was taking the easy way out. Maybe he'd rather get an amputation over with now rather than have to battle operation after operation so my dad could keep his leg. These were understandable thoughts, and they were thoughts that my mom, my brother, and I had and that we discussed.

But suppose that Dr. Frasco had come to my family and said that during the operation, my dad was going to need a significant number of blood transfusions, and that they were having trouble finding a suitable donor. And suppose further that Dr. Frasco—out of compassion for my father and for my family—offered to donate his own blood. And suppose even further that Dr. Frasco did this at the risk of his own life, perhaps because such a large quantity of blood was needed.

Now, in this situation, my response to Dr. Frasco would change markedly. Maybe I couldn't explain to you the *reasons* why Dr. Frasco might have to amputate my dad's leg, and maybe initially I had reason to be suspicious of his prognosis.

But if Dr. Frasco had offered my dad his own blood, I would have been convinced that he was for us. I would have been convinced that we could trust him, and I would have been rightly convinced of this. Even if Dr. Frasco's reasoning remained opaque to me, he would have done something so loving that I could only rationally conclude that he was for us.

The Christian claim is that this is precisely what God has done for each of us. When He saw us hurting and in need of healing, He provided His own blood. He chose to join us in our suffering and to take on Himself whatever suffering was necessary for us to be healed. He displayed His love in such an extravagant way that we have strong reason to trust Him, even when we don't fully understand His ways.

The Cross of Christ

The problem with this response to the objection from suffering is that it assumes that Jesus' suffering and death were an extravagant display of love. But you might think it was *anything but* a display of love.

"Jesus died for you," the Christian says. But what does that actually *mean*? You might ask, "What kind of God would send His Son to die?" It's a very good question. And here is the response Richard Dawkins recommends: the idea of God sending His Son to die is

vicious, sado-masochistic and repellant. We should also dismiss it as barking mad, but for its ubiquitous familiarity which has dulled our objectivity. If God wanted to forgive our sins, why not just forgive them, without having himself tortured and executed in payment[?][2]

I am going to offer a different take on Jesus' death, a take that I hope will explain why Jesus' death—both *how* He died and *why* He died—is understood by Christians to be the ultimate display of God's love for us.

How Jesus Died

First let's look at *how* Jesus died. I was once told, "When you are pushed to your visceral limit, the real you comes out." It always struck me that there is an element of truth in that claim.

When you are in the worst pain, at the point of greatest frustration, when you are insulted and stepped on and then stepped on again. In those moments you learn a lot about yourself. What comes out of me in those times is not always very attractive. What came out of Jesus was love, compassion, and forgiveness.

Though the Roman judge found no basis for a charge against Him, the Jewish leaders insisted Jesus be killed because He claimed to be divine. And so they stripped Him, and beat Him, and strung Him up on a cross—to be shamed publicly and to slowly die one of the most painful deaths possible.

Jesus looked down from that cross at those who were killing Him, and prayed:

Father, forgive them; for they know not what they do.
(Luke 23:34 KJV)

If Jesus forgave even *then*, we can be sure there is no sin He will not forgive, if we will just ask.

Then Jesus turned to His mother and to one of His best friends, and He said to His mother,

"Here is your son," and to the disciple, "Here is your mother." From that time on, this disciple took her into his home. (John 19:26–27)

Even as He hung dying, Jesus was first concerned not with His own life but with His mother's life, and with making sure she would be cared for after He was gone.

And then one of the criminals who was being executed alongside Jesus began to heap insults on Him:

"Aren't you the Messiah? Save yourself and us!"

But the other criminal [on Jesus' other side] rebuked him. "Don't you fear God," he said ... "We are punished justly, for we are getting what our deeds deserve. But this man has done nothing wrong."

Then he said, "Jesus, remember me when you come into your kingdom."

Jesus answered him, "Truly I tell you, today you will be with me in paradise." (Luke 23:39–43)

The final thing Jesus did on the cross—as He was struggling to take His last breaths—was to love the man next to Him (a criminal), and to promise that man salvation in response to his repentant heart and his trust in Him.

It is recorded that "when the centurion, who stood there in front of Jesus, saw how he died, he said, 'Surely this man was the Son of God!'" (Mark 15:39). When they saw *how* Jesus died, they knew that Jesus was divine, because when you are pushed to your limit, the real you comes out. And what came out of Jesus was a display of love that was absolutely divine.

Why Jesus Died

Why was Jesus so perfect in death? Why did He die with such utter integrity? Because that's why He came in the first place. There is no notion in Christianity of Jesus being forced to come and die. As God Himself, Jesus chose to come and live a human life, and He chose to die a human death. Jesus said, "No one takes [my life] from me, but I lay it down of my own accord" (John 10:18).

And even on the cross, voicing those agonizing words, "My God, my God, why have you forsaken me?" (Matthew 27:46; Mark 15:34), Jesus was not only giving expression to the depth of His suffering, but He was also quoting the first verse of Psalm 22—in a sense, asking us to read on. And when we do, what we find is that even from the agony of the cross, Jesus was reminding us that He went to His death knowingly and purposefully. He pointed us to a text written hundreds of years earlier but describing detail after detail of the exact manner of His execution. And Jesus was also reminding us that even amid His experience of utter isolation and estrangement, He maintained His trust that God "has listened to his cry for help" (Psalm 22:24).

But *why*? How Jesus died was remarkable, but *why* did Jesus choose to come, and suffer, and lay down His life? I want to begin to sketch three reasons.[3]

... *For Our Suffering*

First, Jesus came to do one of the only things that can make a difference to someone in the midst of terrible suffering: to join them in their pain and suffer alongside them.

Awhile back I was scrolling around the Facebook page for "Boating and Water Safety"—as you do—and I came across an article claiming that when a ship sinks, women are more likely to die than men. And there was a long online discussion about why this might be the case, but what stuck out to me was one comment by a woman named Kristin, who said, "I am not surprised. A woman with children has probably the least chance of survival. I would rather die with my child than leave my child to die if I could save myself."

Imagine being on a sinking ship, and a young child is stuck in a compartment that is slowly being filled with water. While you can drop down into the compartment from where you are, there is no way to get back out. The child is going to slowly die there. And the little boy or little girl is distraught, and suffering, and scared.

Imagine a parent who lowers herself into the compartment, knowing that it will mean her death, too, just to be with the child in his suffering—to comfort him and to ensure that he will not die alone.

I would rather die *with* my child than leave my child to die if I could save myself.

Is that such a "barking mad" thing to do? Not if you have a child. My wife and I have amazing godchildren: Sophia,

Aiden, Mia, and Carys. And when we look at them and hold them, we get it. We understand. It might seem foolish to make this sacrifice in many instances, but not for the people you cherish most.

What does that say, then, about who we must be to God— to a God who would rather suffer *with* us than not suffer without us?

John Stott identified the parental love of God as well as anyone:

I could never myself believe in God, if it were not for the cross. The only God I believe in is the One Nietzsche ridiculed as "God on the cross." In the real world of pain, how could one worship a God who was immune to it?

I have entered many Buddhist temples in different Asian countries and stood respectfully before the statue of the Buddha, his legs crossed, arms folded, eyes closed, the ghost of a smile playing round his mouth, a remote look on his face, detached from the agonies of the world.

But each time after a while I have had to turn away. And in imagination I have turned instead to that lonely, twisted, tortured figure on the cross, nails through hands and feet, back lacerated, limbs wrenched, brow bleeding from thorn-pricks, mouth dry and intolerably thirsty, plunged in God-forsaken darkness.

That is the God for me! He laid aside His immunity to pain. He entered our world of flesh and blood, tears and death. He suffered for us.

Our sufferings become more manageable in the light of His. There is still a question mark against human suffering, but over it we boldly stamp another mark, the cross that symbolizes divine suffering.[4]

Jesus was ridiculed while He was on the cross: "He saved others; let him save himself" (Luke 23:35).

And with the heart of a parent, Jesus responded by preferring to die with His children rather than leave His children to die and save Himself.

That is one reason why Jesus died, and why His death was a display of utmost love.

... For Our Sin

But Jesus' ultimate reason for suffering and dying on the cross was to save humanity from our sin, to take our just punishment on Himself, so that we could be free.

We sometimes work hard to avoid admitting that we're sinful. I was reminded of this a few years back when I applied for a visa to take a job in England. And on the official form, in order not to get deported, I had to answer no to this question: "Have you or any dependents who are applying with you ever engaged in any other activities which might indicate that you may not be considered to be persons of good character?"

I just cracked up laughing when I read that. It might as well have read "Have you ever done *anything* wrong?" (And people say America is tough on immigration!)

If you want proof that we're sinful, one of the best ways to get it is to turn out the lights. Sin is what we do in the dark, when no one is watching.

Like if you go to the theater to see a movie, and you get a nice big bucket of popcorn. You walk into the theater as a normal human being...and then the lights dim, and out of nowhere you become a complete slob.

First you assume the slob position—you slouch forward in your chair, place your bucket of popcorn on your stomach, and open your mouth as wide as you can—and then you just start flicking popcorn in the general direction of your mouth, not really caring if it lands in. Or you take the biggest handful of popcorn possible, and even though you know that there is *no way* all of it could possibly fit into your mouth, you try anyway! And you spill about half of it down your shirt and onto the floor.

When there's nothing left in your bucket, you start eating popcorn off your shirt and your jeans and down the crevices in your seat. (You know you do it!) And then when the movie's over, since the lights are still dimmed, we just leave our mess for someone else to clean up!

It's amazing what happens when we know others can't see. You wouldn't act like that in the light. You wouldn't act like that over dinner on a first date. You wouldn't ask your date, "Mind if I try your potato?" and then just reach over and toss potato in the general vicinity of your mouth, leaving half of it on your jeans for later.

But here's the thing: The "light of the world" (John 8:12; 9:5), Jesus, sees us even in the darkness. And He sees not only the popcorn that misses our mouths, but how we think of other people, what we say behind their backs, the things we choose to look at, how we spend money.

There was a boy named Eric whom I used to fight with as a teenager. He wasn't a very nice kid, and I welcomed opportunities to put him down. A few years ago I heard that Eric had killed himself.

"For the wages of sin is death" (Romans 6:23). Never have those words been more real to me than when I heard this news. Would he have killed himself if I had been kind to him? If I had offered my hand to him?

I don't know.

Sometimes when I try to explain sin to people they want to tell me I'm exaggerating, that really I'm pretty good—it's not like I've "killed" anyone.

Yes, I have. And what if God shone His light not just on Eric but on the rippling effects of all of my unkind words over the years, and on all of those whom I could have helped with time and resources that I squandered on my own luxury instead? I am undoubtedly in need of a Savior.

I can remember things I used to do—like the way I treated Eric—that at the time I thought were no big deal, but that now I can recognize as truly terrible. Now that God has led me away from some of those things, I can look back and see how ugly they really were. And I'm *right* about those things now. I was *wrong* then. It's only because I've left behind some of those things that now I can look back and see them for what they truly were.

Well, imagine how far along this path God is. I've taken minimal steps at best. God would have the perfect perspective. His perspective would be the true one, and none of us would look very holy from there. In fact, Jesus tells us something of what sin looks like from God's perspective: lusting for another's spouse like adultery;[5] hate like murder.[6]

Sometimes it's hard for us to appreciate the truth about our own sin until we encounter someone holier than ourselves. My wife once wrote out a list for me of forty things that no one else knew about her that she wanted me to know before we got engaged. Jo wanted to make sure that I desired to step into marriage with all of her, and not only what had been brought out in the light. It was a beautiful thing to do. Traumatizing! But beautiful.

And so Jo talked me through this list. And when we got down to #19, Jo said, "Now this one I'm really ashamed of. I really feel I've betrayed your trust and this may be the *worst* thing I've *ever* done to you."

At this point I'm trying to keep a calm appearance, but I'm flipping out. You can just imagine the things running through my mind: *She's cheated on me. She's a spy and has to kill me because I know too much. She's secretly a Red Sox fan!*

And then Jo explained that one day when we were already looking at photos on my computer—together—and I stepped out of the room to answer the front door, she merely continued perusing the files on my computer to look at old photos of me. And I thought to myself, *You've got to be kidding! Photo stalking?! That's the* worst *thing you've* ever *done to me?! Oh man, I'm in so much trouble!*

Our sin is magnified by the goodness of the person in whose presence we are standing. That's why when the criminal who hung next to Jesus saw the holiness with which Jesus died, he knew that his own punishment was just. That's why

Christians believe that on the day we stand in God's presence, all of us will be able to recognize our need for a Savior.

The staggering news of the Christian faith is that God loved us too much to let us bear the judgment for our sins ourselves. But how exactly does Jesus' death help matters? It is the *guilty* who are responsible for their sins. If instead Jesus suffered the consequences, how is that justice?

Say I get a bit nostalgic for my boxing days and severely assault you by throwing punches in your direction. It would hardly make you, as the victim, think I had been justly dealt with if I pointed out that some other guy, who had nothing to do with my assaulting you, had been sent to jail for my crime instead! It's hard to see how that would be a display of love, or of justice. And that is how Christianity is sometimes perceived.

But let's change the scenario. What if I began hitting you, but then when I went to hit you again, my wife, Jo, threw herself in the way to try to stop it, and my punch hit her, and sent her head flying back into a stone wall, and it killed her? And when I saw the consequences of my action for the one I love dearly, I broke down in agony in front of you, and pleaded for forgiveness.

Would you still feel that justice had not been served for my sin against you? I suspect not. Why? Because what could be worse for me than losing the person I love most, and at my own hands. Nothing could be more severe. It would be callous and cruel to demand more.

On the cross, God threw Himself between us and each person we have ever wronged. In an overflow of love, He took the full impact of our sins. He suffered our punishment.

But that doesn't mean there are no consequences for us. We face the consequences of seeing our sins result in the death of our Creator and of the One who loves us most. It's when we understand this that we fall to our knees in repentance and ask for forgiveness. And yet because Jesus is risen, because death could not hold Him (Acts 2:24), our repentance is turned not to the agony of seeing a loved one die, but to the pure joy of receiving a loved one back from the dead.

The objection that Jesus' death on our behalf is unjust rests on the assumption that Jesus' death is disconnected from us, irrelevant to our sins, just some stranger serving our jail sentence. But that is true only if Jesus is in fact a stranger to us. If we are indifferent to Jesus, if we have no interest in following Him, then His death *is* as the death of a stranger, someone we don't know serving our sentence. And there is no justice in that. Then we are still under judgment. Then justice remains to be fulfilled in the life to come.

But if we love Jesus, if we put our trust in Him and choose to follow Him, then when we stand beneath the cross and see the death of the person we love most resulting from our sin, just consequences have occurred. Then the cross is anything but disconnected; it has every relevance to us. Justice has been fulfilled.

Jesus took the consequences that lead to death so that we could take the consequences that lead to repentance, and to freedom, and to eternal life.

That's just one partial analogy of what God did at the cross. No analogy could capture it in full. But I find this analogy helpful in showing that what happened at the cross in no way undermined justice. In fact, quite the opposite.

Some of you reading this book have been treated very badly. You've been on the receiving end of far too many punches. And that matters to God.

The cross is where God protested that it's *not okay* to just look the other way when people are beaten, and abused, and enslaved, that there *do* have to be serious consequences for sin. But the cross is also where God declared that He can't stand to see any of those He has brought into this world lose their lives to those consequences. And so He lost His own life, and in doing so offered to every person a life that can never be lost.

God looked down as a parent from heaven and saw His children fighting with one another—killing one another. And He did what a loving parent would do. He threw Himself between them. And *He* took the punch, and *He* suffered the death, so that they could live.

More amazing still is the fact that God responds this way even though we haven't just been fighting with each other, but with God Himself. Every time we throw a punch—whether literally, or by words, or by indifference—we fight against God, too, because we throw a punch at someone He loves. And our fighting is also directly against God, because so often we prefer to be our own gods—when we know what God wants, when we know that He knows best, and yet we deny Him anyway. The deepest betrayal is sin against the One who loves you best. And though time and again we deny Him, at the cross God chose us. Love at its very best.

Justice demands judgment. Love demands mercy. Only at the cross of Jesus do we find both. Only at the cross do we find perfect love and perfect justice in perfect intersection. That is why Jesus came. That is why Jesus was ready to die.

...For Our Shame

Jesus died for our suffering; He died for our sin; and finally, He died for our shame.

Just when I thought I had gotten past the worst in the list of "40 Things No One Knows About Jo," she hit me with #37. It was only four words, but four words you think you'll never hear from your significant other:

"I am a Trekkie."

That's right; Jo loves *Star Trek*.

This is something very few people know about Jo—well, until this book was published. Oops. She had done a pretty good job hiding this embarrassing fact from me early in our dating relationship, and I still think the only reason she told me was because a new *Star Trek* movie had come out in theaters and therefore she *had* to tell me so that I would take her to see it. (Jo recalls reasoning that one of the few things more embarrassing than being a *Star Trek* fan would be going to see a *Star Trek* movie by herself!)

So Jo read me #37, and I could tell when she did that she thought I would think less of her for it. Others had mocked her about this when she was young, and so she thought she had reason to be ashamed.

We arranged to meet at the movies, and when Jo got there, I was standing out front proudly wearing a T-shirt of Mr. Spock's face that read "Live long and prosper." And I was holding open a massive *Star Trek* poster that charged all passers-by "To Boldly Go Where No Man Has Gone Before!"

But as Jo approached me she had tears in her eyes, and she

threw her arms around me for the biggest hug. And that's when I started to understand that for me to literally *wear* Jo's embarrassment somehow freed her from having to be embarrassed. And I told her, "I will never be ashamed of you, so you never need to be ashamed of yourself."

God used a funny T-shirt and a ridiculous poster to teach me and Jo something very significant about Him that night. Jesus died not only for our sin; He died also for our shame.

I don't know about you, but I know that for both me and Jo, some of the hardest memories for us to shake are ones of when we've been shamed. Maybe a time we were mocked, or ignored, or treated like objects rather than persons. Sometimes even just a couple of words, and they can weigh on us for *years*—words that say "You're ugly," "You're not good enough," "You're not worth the time."

Naked on the cross, Jesus took upon Himself every time we've been mocked, every time we've been spit on, every time we've failed. He took upon Himself every time we've been abused, exposed, ignored, overlooked. When He put on human flesh,[7] Jesus literally *clothed* Himself in all of it.

Some object that the idea of a divine person dying is shameful. They are correct. It is full of *our* shame. Jesus wore our shame so that, as the Bible says, "Anyone who believes in him will never be put to shame" (Romans 10:11; cf. Psalm 25:3). And again:

> "Do not be afraid; you will not be put to shame. Do not
> fear disgrace; you will not be humiliated. You will forget

the shame of your youth"...Instead of your shame you will receive a double portion, and instead of disgrace you will rejoice in your inheritance...and everlasting joy will be yours. (Isaiah 54:4; 61:7)

On the cross, Jesus proclaimed that when you put your trust in Him you don't have to be ashamed of whatever you've been through, because He's been through it, too. He hung vulnerable and rejected in a shameful way so that we would never again need to live in shame.

The cross was God's public proclamation to the whole world that you are deeply loved and eternally desired—as Paul put it, created to be God's *poiēma*, His poem, His "masterpiece."[8] And therefore, as Eleonore Stump concludes,

> No matter what the standard is with respect to which a person is shamed, that standard is trumped by the standard constituted by loving relationship with God...In virtue of being desired by the most powerful and most good being possible, a human person is desirable by the ultimate of all standards. By *this* standard, then, all shame has to fall away.[9]

It has to fall away because God's standard—the ultimate standard—shames all of the false standards that threaten to shame us. And by the measure of God's standard—the standard won by Jesus on the cross—God disrobes us of our shame, and He dresses us in acceptance, confidence, honor, and inheritance.

A God We Can Trust

There is a depth of relationship that is possible only between people who have been through the worst together—those who have been there in each other's darkest times, those who have fought through disaster side by side, those who have sat beside each other in devastation with nothing left to say. Because of Jesus, and because of what Jesus accomplished on the cross, that depth of relationship is possible with God.

I have used various analogies to communicate something of the love that was expressed by God on the cross. The danger with analogies is that they are never perfect—they are inevitably disanalogous in some respects and emphasize certain aspects more than others. Nevertheless, it is my hope that these analogies have grasped at a number of important responses to the question at hand: *Why* did Jesus choose to come and die?

> To suffer alongside us when we suffer.
> To offer forgiveness for our sins.
> To offer freedom from our shame.

> What kind of God would come and die?

> A God of love. A God we can trust.

If we understand what happened two thousand years ago on a Friday afternoon, at the wooden cross that Jesus died on, we will understand why we can trust God amid suffering. For "greater love has no one than this: to lay down one's life for one's friends" (John 15:13).

In both *how* He died and *why* He died, Jesus presented to us an extravagant and unparalleled display of love. He is the surgeon who is willing to give up His life to heal what threatens our lives—suffering, sin, shame. He is the doctor who is willing to die so that His patients might live. And therefore we can trust Him.

We can trust Him because His display of love is overriding evidence that there is a good explanation for the allowance of suffering, even when we are not in a position to understand that explanation in full.

Someone might object that this response to the problem of suffering assumes distinctively Christian beliefs about the divinity of Jesus. That's true, but if it is the existence of the *Christian* God that is being challenged, then Christians have to be allowed to make use of Christian beliefs in their response. If, on the other hand, the worldview that is being critiqued is not one that claims the divinity of Jesus, then Christians can simply agree that whatever god is being objected to does not exist.

If all I told you about my childhood front-yard football career was that my mom yelled at me to get back in the game when I was crying and wanted to quit, you would be excused for questioning whether I had a caring mother. But that was not the whole story.

When my mom reflects back on that memorable day, she remembers that all she wanted to do was pick me up and carry me inside and wrap me up in the safety of her arms. But she also knew that if I were to become the person I was supposed to become, she could not always keep me safe. And so she *did* send me back into that game. But not without suffering alongside me, not without bleeding with me (even bleeding because of me), not without doing whatever it took to empower me to face the suffering before me.

When I tell you the *full* story, you know my mom is *for me*; you know her care is beyond question. For a parent who is willing to bend down and suffer herself is a parent who can be trusted amid suffering. And when we consider not just theism in the abstract, but the full story of Christianity, we find a God who has bent down and done precisely that.

~&~

CHAPTER 5

OTHER RESPONSES ON OFFER: BUDDHISM, ISLAM, NATURALISM

Ravi Zacharias

"Give me the making of the songs of a nation," said eighteenth-century Scottish political thinker Andrew Fletcher, "and I care not who writes its laws."[1] Considering that this was written decades before our capacity for the mass distribution of ideas, his statement is amazingly perceptive regarding how *felt* realities hit home harder than the strictures of logic or argument.

Feelings will often trump argument if the one doing the feeling senses that the one responding with answers is completely detached from their pain. Laws, be they in legal terms or in the area of logic, often have the appearance of being separated from the heart. Music, on the other hand, flows from the passions of longing and need. People tend to find a law helpful only if it protects them. Music and lyrics provide expression for the cries of virtually every civilization. Can the two ever meet?

I have often wondered if one of the differences between the

animal kingdom and human beings is not merely in essence and in propositional proclivities but also in the ability to create music. But that is just an aside, and I won't head down that path now.

The question for us here is, Can reason and feeling come together so that the one addresses the other in a persuasion of the mind and the heart? Reason, of course, in this instance will argue for the place of legitimate laws within which life is described. The larger challenge is whether law can ever be seen as a good thing, not just for one individual but for all of humanity. In other words, can I be convinced of its benefit even if it creates pain for me for the moment? (That is difficult because law is more often seen as restrictive and threatening than as liberating and protecting.) Is it possible to legitimately distance one's self from emotion so as to grasp the argument? Is there a way for argument to capture the emotion, to not be seen as distant from the emotion of the pain?

The book of Psalms is preached from more often than any other book in the Bible. In the pages of the Psalms, pain and sorrow are addressed repeatedly by various poets. King David wrote about the emotional distress and fears with which he lived in numerous songs and poems that prefigured Shakespeare in their grasp of human tragedy and the machinations of the human heart.

Yet David wrote in equal terms of the benefit of the law of God and of his love for the law. What ought to have been and what was fill the pages of the book of Psalms. I am convinced that musicians are able to raise the appropriate questions in the most potent terms and at the same time hint at the answers in the most real terms.

Years ago, Justin Hayward and the Moody Blues sang a song they titled "Question":

Why do we never get an answer
When we're knocking at the door
With a thousand million questions
About hate and death and war?
'Cause when we stop and look around us
There is nothing that we need,
In a world of persecution that is whirling in its greed.
Why do we never get an answer
When we're knocking at the door?
Because the truth is hard to swallow
That's what the war of love is for.[2]

These are the haunting questions of the soul. One might readily counter the lyricist by asking, "But haven't you read the responses of various philosophers to the question? Haven't you seen how many answers there are? How can you say that you never get an answer? Have you never plumbed the depths of the writings of old, be they biblical or of other religions or philosophical dissertations?"

The songwriter will remain unfazed because to the average person the questions are really not of a philosophical or even a logical nature; rather, answering the questions is more like trying to reconcile all the pieces of a puzzle. In the human mind, there are aspects of this puzzle that bring discomfort such as pain, which is present in even attempting an answer to the question.

The question of pain is an enormous one. It is easy to give

answers when it is someone else's pain and very difficult to philosophize when the pain is your own. C. S. Lewis wrote a powerful work on the problem of pain.[3] Yet, when he lost his wife, his book *A Grief Observed* moved the struggle from the third person to the first. The difference in the emotional tug was unmistakable. I remember a publisher telling me once of a particular writer whose books, in his view, were written for his own personal therapy, hoping in the writing for a catharsis. I'm sure that is not uncommon.

In this subject of pain and suffering, more than any other, the fist is clenched either in an honest effort to find answers or in the dark private moments of pain. How can any power justify itself as beneficent when the weakest among us experience unexplainable pain before they've even had a chance at life? That form of the question moves it away from mere argument to immediacy and purpose, and those two components are very hard to satisfy. Can experiencing pain now for the benefit of some ultimate purpose in the future satisfy us in the moment?

This book is written in an effort to answer the questions of these conflicting issues. The responses we have offered to this point are centered on freedom, grace, and forgiveness— realities that address the questions of the mind, but while speaking to the heart.

In this chapter I will look at how a number of other worldviews approach the question of pain and suffering, and I will express why I believe the Christian answer is the only one that not only meets the test of logic and corresponds to heartfelt reality, but that also meaningfully justifies the question. That justification is important, and, frankly, I am not at all convinced that the naturalist can even justify the question he is asking.

That is an important beginning point. A *Far Side* comic strip some years ago depicted a ballroom at a butlers' convention, crowded with attendees all attired in their tuxedos. At one side of the room, and the focus of everyone's attention, was a dead butler on the floor, while a detective in the picture muttered, "I hate to begin a Monday with a case like this." If the classic line for finger-pointing in any crime is "The butler did it," then it goes without saying that a murder at a butlers' convention does not quite expedite a solution.

In a universe that owes its beginning to God, simply saying that God allows pain and suffering does not help. On the other hand, in a universe that is purely random, there is no way to justify calling pain and suffering evil. What does the term even mean in such a universe? Hence, we must fine-tune the question. Why suffering? Why do we experience pain?

I propose a multi-framed panel that has to be studied to gain some understanding of this puzzle. After turning to these panels in sequence, we might see our way clearer to understanding the distinctiveness of the Christian response to our question when set alongside other responses on offer.

As Real as Life Itself: Suffering Is a Reality

The famed writer Gabriel Marcel made a profound statement describing evil not as a problem but as a mystery. Was he dodging the question? Hardly. He went on to explain that "a mystery is a problem that encroaches on its own data."[4]

"Getting to Mars is a problem," Peter Kreeft adds, but "falling in love is a mystery."[5] Why is that so? Because a mystery is a problem that encroaches upon itself.

What does that mean? It means that finding a solution to a problem of which we ourselves are inextricably a part is difficult if we do not recognize our own role in it. That makes it a mystery. A problem just needs a solution. A mystery needs an explanation. With that in mind, let us move forward.

There are two ways in which a problem encroaches upon itself. The first is clearly by way of prejudice. Suppose a young man is charged with a crime. Witnesses to the crime describe what happened. But when his mother takes the stand, she testifies to the innocence of her son. First, she tries to change the facts. Seeing she is heading nowhere, she resorts to discrediting the accusers by offering different motives for her son's actions. Can her testimony be taken seriously or will her own motives be suspect for obvious reasons? She has become part of the problem, and the jury has to go with the facts.

But prejudice is not the only way a problem encroaches upon itself. Suppose an umpire in a baseball game is following the line of the ball as carefully as he can and calls a ball a fair catch, not seeing that it was trapped against the wall. He can believe with absolute certainty that the catch was made. But when it is discovered later that he was in the early stages of myopia and just didn't see clearly enough, his physical limitation cannot be used to accuse him of the prejudice of bias, even though the outcome is the same as if he had made the call based on bias.

Errors in judgment can be made both from bias and because of an inner shortcoming. That is why a problem is easier to solve than a mystery; there is a theory attached to solving a problem. A mystery is more difficult to understand because there is so much potential for it to be compromised. The facts may not change, but identifying who is involved in the telling is critical. With that backdrop we face the mystery.

First, suffering is real. Need one even argue this point? But just in case we forget, there are some religions that actually do try to dispense with suffering as illusion or as a scenario being staged for the benefit of an audience while behind the curtain all is well. In my years of traveling the world, I have seen much suffering and have often had no recourse but silence in the presence of someone going through agonies. If suffering were not real, most of the religions in the world would not even exist. If it were not real, the skeptic would have no ax to grind against theism. The reality of suffering is inescapable.

I mentioned that I underwent major back surgery. I had herniated a couple of disks, and after suffering for many years with constant pain, I went under the surgeon's blade. Anyone who has gone through major back surgery can testify to its rigors. The surgeon performed a triple fusion and installed hardware to brace the vertebrae from L3 to the sacrum. How well I recall even months after the surgery pulling up in front of a restaurant one night to join my family for dinner and the pain in my lower back being so intense that I just put my head on the steering wheel and wept.

For years I lived with this. I avoided medication because I had heard and seen that what begins as a solution often ends up becoming the problem. So I endured the pain.

Physical pain and the emotional and spiritual brokenness that often eclipse physical pain are the twin carriers of suffering. Our physical and emotional makeup provide the tracks for our agonies. They are the physical carriers to the brain, but the mind goes beyond the physical and the emotional to raise the question of pain itself. One look at the list of specialties at any hospital or psychology clinic will show that "Pain Management" is obviously a well-staffed discipline. Add to that the stresses of raising a family or what one hears on the news every night. Suffering? It is as real as life itself.

As Vast as the World: Suffering Is Universal

I have learned to listen to questions very carefully because words and sentiments reveal deeper thought and feeling. Are there any clues that something deeper is at issue, even in the way the question of suffering is framed? Note, for example, the words of David Hume:

Were a stranger to drop suddenly into this world I would show him as a specimen of its ills, a hospital full of diseases, a prison crowded with malefactors and debtors, a field strewn with carcasses, a fleet floundering in the ocean, a nation languishing under tyranny, famine and pestilence. To a ball, to an opera, to court? He might justly think that I was only showing him a diversity of distress and sorrow.[6]

Here is the cry of another:

It is not science that has led me to doubt the purpose of God. It is the state of the world. It is this pitiless unending

struggle for existence among the nations. It is the collapse of our idealisms before the brute facts of force and
chaos...that there is a radical twist in the very consti-
tution of the universe which will always defeat man's
hopes, make havoc of his dreams and bring his pathetic
optimism crashing in disaster. Purpose? Look at the
world. That settles it for me.[7]

These two statements together summarize the predicament.
In the second we see the pursuit of recognizing any purpose
to life questioned because of the universality of suffering.
What purpose can there be to life in the face of such pain?
And in the first, Hume goes beyond the question of just purpose to insinuate a question of love: How can there be a *loving*
purpose in a world full of "distress and sorrow"? His litany
of woes demands a twin explanation for purpose and love. It
seems inadequate to just ask, What purpose is there in this?
The follow-up question is, How can this be justified as love?

This is interesting and clearly a cultural distinctive of the
way the West positions the problem of suffering and evil.
While the problem is universal, how it is positioned within
a worldview framework is not uniform. In the West, the
difficulty behind the question is juxtaposing overall purpose
and love. In the East, the problem is stated so that the focus
is on the cause of a specific suffering and how to eliminate it.

This difference is fascinating to me because even though
the problem is expressed in the West in philosophical or
theoretical terms of overall purpose and love, pain is dealt
with in a very physical way, with hospitals, counselors, medi-
cines, rescue missions, and the like. It was in the West that

an anesthetic that eliminated pain was discovered. When Sir James Simpson first administered chloroform during childbirth, it was initially reported that the delighted woman called her new daughter Anaesthesia. The name of the baby was later disputed, saying that Anaesthesia was a nickname Simpson used for the child. But it is true that upon awakening from the anesthetic, the woman did not believe she had given birth.

Masking pain was a step forward for surgery. The West has rightly gone to great lengths to reduce the agony of putting a blade to the body. The volumes of philosophy books written in the West on the subject of pain and suffering, as well as the universities educating the masses into asking the question at such a lofty level, all have in mind the end game of skepticism or even atheism. The mitigation of pain in the physical world is seen as an advance, but the spiritual strength that enables a person to persevere in the face of pain is considered unreal and is belittled.

In the East, the conclusion that is drawn about pain and suffering is often fatalistic and, rather than seeking to bring physical relief, is either totally spiritualized or used to develop a philosophy that attempts to see some good in it all. In all the years of addressing audiences across cultures, until recently I had never heard the connection between the question of suffering and God's existence raised in the East. I myself marveled that the existence of God was a nonissue in the face of such grand-scale suffering.

Only in recent times, with the huge devastation of the Japanese tsunami in 2011 and more recently the typhoon in the Philippines, have such questions been broached. And even then, it is more often the Western-trained journalists or educators who posit the question that way, possibly reflecting the unification of our thinking through mass media and an overall challenge to ancient thinking that makes the contemporary seem more realistic.

For the masses still, it is not the question of the existence of God that is raised but the question of Job—the why of it all. Whether in the East or the West, the reality of pain and suffering is universally granted, but the context is very different.

Let us take a deeper look at three of the major views arising from various contexts.

1. Buddhism: "Whatever"

After seeing sickness, old age, death, and asceticism, Gautama Buddha found as his answer to suffering the life of renunciation and the elimination of desire. His questions about sickness, old age, and death led to his own asceticism, though he still felt that no one had really answered the questions. So he pursued his quest for the answers to suffering and pain with total abandon by rejecting the world and reflecting, meditating, and pondering the why of it all.

The word that he used is *dukha*. It is not an uncommon word in the languages that come from Sanskrit and is used both at the popular and at the more formal level of language. *Sukh* means comfort and well-being; *dukh* means anguish and sorrow and pain. Buddha reached a climactic conclusion that the source of the problem lay in "desire." Take, for example, the family. Your attachments and affections for them will inevitably bring pain. Myriad sufferings come to you because you are joined to them in affection.

So the Buddhist cure is simple but lifelong: If you do not desire anything, you will not be hurt when anything is taken from you. Kill desire and attachment, and you kill pain and suffering. That is why the life of a monk is enjoined for a short period of time by many in the East to taste renunciation and experience life apart from the attachments of this world, which will only trap you; and, once trapped, you will be forced to repeat the same quest in the next life. Each life is a rebirth and each rebirth is a payment for previous wrongs. The goal is to stop wanting anything. The old English adage says, "If wishes were horses, beggars would ride." Buddhism would say, "If wishes were eliminated, there would be no need for a horse or a ride."

The entire corpus of material in Buddhism is summarized in four subheadings.

1. The fact of suffering
2. The cause of suffering
3. The cessation of suffering
4. The path to that cessation

Simply stated, suffering results from past actions and from the reality of desire. We desire things; we desire circumstances; we desire success; we desire wealth; we desire happiness. All these desires make us pursue habits and make decisions that we think will help us get "there," but that also make us vulnerable to pain and suffering.

And in the end, in this life we never get "there." Instead, we find ourselves in a state in which our desire only grows. We need to find a "there" where we will no longer desire anything—the state of *nirvana*, where we do not will or want anything because the will has been extinguished.

The conclusion this produces, apart from the obvious contradiction, is that detachment is the key to happiness. But even there, it is not so much happiness as it is a sublime form of apathy. Think about it. You simply do not wish for anything anymore, and so you are never without what you wish to have. If pain were a clenched fist, the will would be air. The fist can keep pounding to no avail. Is it really possible to reach such a state and yet remain human?

Some years ago, I was in Thailand and spent time with the first ordained woman monk in that country. Since Thai Buddhism doesn't ordain women, she had gone to Sri Lanka to be ordained. She also had a PhD degree from a prestigious university in Canada. As we sat across from each other at a table, I offered her some mango pudding that I had brought as a gift for her, though I wasn't sure she would accept it because I was aware of the strictures upon her as a monk. She did, but she told me that since it was past one o'clock in the afternoon, she couldn't touch it or any food until the next morning, so if I would kindly put it directly into her bag where she could access it later rather than hand it to her, she would appreciate it.

Our conversation began.

"I hear you have a family," I said.

"Yes, I am not with my husband anymore, but I have children."

"Are you able to see them often?"

"Yes, I pick them up from school every afternoon before I return to my temple base."

"How do you pick them up?"

"I have my own car."

"Oh! I didn't know you could have your own car."

"Normally we don't, and technically someone else should drive me. But because I'm a woman and can't be in a car alone with a man, I drive myself."

"So you do not spend the night with your children?"

"No."

"Is that hard on you?"

A hesitation, a surge of emotion, an obvious struggle, and then the answer: "It's very hard. But I'm working on it."

"Working on what?"

"Working on not feeling this way and on not missing them."

"So the goal would be to not desire a relationship with your children, right?"

"Yes."

"I find that interesting, because the night Gautama Buddha left his home was the very night his son was born."

"That is correct."

"So he, too, relinquished his family and his home."

"That's right."

"Who would you say best represents that state of no desire at present?"

"I would say the Dalai Lama."

"But he speaks out for the liberation of Tibet...isn't that a desire?"

"You could say that."

"But is that a noble desire?"

"You will have to ask him."

"Why do you think he desires that when he knows it is that very desire that keeps him from attaining the goal of life?"

Pause…pause…pause. "Let's just say it's because he chooses to."

"So the will to liberate Tibet trumps the will to want nothing?"

A tilted shake of the head. "May I switch to another question?"

"If you wish. What do you think brings about all this suffering?"

"Desire."

"Do we inherit this from our past?"

"Yes."

"So every birth is a rebirth."

"Yes."

"And this present birth is a finite number, don't you think?"

"I am not sure what you mean."

"Well, starting from now, if you count back, you will arrive at a finite number."

"That is correct."

"So you had a first birth."

"Yes."

"What desire did you inherit at your first birth?"

"We do not ask such questions."

"I'm sorry. I just thought I would ask."

Our conversation proceeded from there till I shared my story of how I came to the knowledge of Jesus Christ and the reality that I confronted in knowing Him. She listened carefully. We parted as she left for her car and I felt sad as she walked away. Denying desire and failing to explain the very origin of pain in life leads one to sit in silence with a smile on one's face in an individually attained apathetic bliss.

One of my closest friends in my undergraduate days was a Canadian of Dutch roots, Koos Fietje. Koos was a remarkable man and intensely persuaded of the necessity of taking the gospel to the neediest of people. He went to the countryside in Thailand, the land of beautiful smiles and a famous saying, "Mai pen rai." Best translated but not quite as cavalier, it means "Never mind." The Australian equivalent is, "She'll be right, mate." The modern-day millennial generation equivalent would be "Whatever."

As Koos preached and taught the truths of the gospel in this land that he loved, he one day paid with his life when an angered Thai was waiting for him as he came out of a prayer meeting and shot him at point-blank range. When the news came back to us all, we were in a state of shock. He left behind a young wife and several young children.

The attitude of some in Thailand was, "Well, he reaped his karma," the same reaction some had when a busload of Westerners were involved in a fatal accident; villagers leaped into the bus and started rummaging through the personal belongings of the victims, looting them of all that was theirs. Their reasoning was that this was karma—their just due; they must have deserved the accident, and there was nothing wrong in taking the spoils of an abstract moral law.

Koos's brother followed in his footsteps and picked up the work he left. To say that the local people in that town were utterly amazed is an understatement. About twenty-five years later, through the generosity of some friends, I was able to help Koos's daughter return to the scene where her father was killed. She had been just a little girl when it happened. Now she was a young mother herself.

And as it turned out, when she sat down in the little church that her father had planted, the lady sitting next to her engaged her in a conversation and realized that she was the daughter of the man who had started the church. Stunned, she told Martina that it had been her husband who had paid for the assassination of her dad. In the intervening years the woman had come to terms with her share in the wrongdoing; she had committed her life to Jesus Christ and sought forgiveness for the tragic murder of a good man.

Every part of her story told of a total paradigm shift: from karma to confession; from fatalism to choice; from indifference to repentance; from nontheism to a personal relationship with God; from escapism to living with the sharp edges of reality. The difference in her life came from a total shift in her thinking, from believing in an abstract moral law to knowing the real personal character of a loving God. Purpose, responsibility, and all else had followed. Does the starting point matter? Yes, it does.

Now let's take a look at how Islam deals with pain and suffering.

2. Islam: Submission Without Questions

Interestingly, Islam has a completely different take on the theme of suffering, but when systematized it comes perilously close to the pantheistic tendencies of Buddhism. I cannot resist a lighter note as I begin this section. Some years ago, I was attending my first cricket match in twenty years. The venue was the historic Wanderers Stadium in Johannesburg. South Africa had emerged from its dark days of apartheid and once again fielded its great cricket team in a championship series.

The day I went to see the game, Pakistan was playing the West Indies. Early in the innings, as Pakistan put in their finest bowler (equivalent to a pitching ace in baseball), the star West Indian batsman took one step forward and hammered the ball a massive distance. All eyes watched the ball sail out of the playing field. In cricketing terms it is called a "six" and was truly a sight to behold. In baseball terms it would be like hitting a whopper of a home run off the first pitch.

As soon as the ball was seen heading out of reach of any player's hands, a large, irate Pakistani fan behind me stood up, clenched his fist toward his own team, and shouted, "That's what you get for playing during Ramadan!" If I weren't putting my own jaw at risk, I would have asked, "What are you doing paying to come and see a game during Ramadan?" It is amazing how size dictates our candor. So I just smiled and looked at my host and knew we had just been entertained more by the fan than by his team. Losing the game because they played at Ramadan may well occupy some conversations around a Muslim table.

Moving away from the lighthearted, let's be serious. After the tragic events of 9/11, I was in a taxi in a Muslim country when the taxi driver asked me, "Are you from America?"

"I'm originally from India, but now America is my home," I said.

"What do you think of what happened in New York when their buildings were destroyed?" He chuckled.

"What do *you* think?" I countered.

His smile turned to anger. "Allah gave us success and punished America!" he replied.

I said, "That is so interesting. What should I say if someone

OTHER RESPONSES ON OFFER • 123

asked me about the plane that was heading to another destination, possibly the White House? That plane crashed without
succeeding in its mission. Who was being punished there?"

There was an ominous silence and a grunt. His glare at me
in the rearview mirror told me this was not a happy thought
for him and possibly for me. But it spoke volumes. These
are not off-the-cuff remarks. Comments like this are "soul-
embraced" beliefs. Everything boils down to "You did this so
God did that." The entire issue of judgment in Islam is one of
being "weighed in the balances" and nothing more than that.

Even in the Old Testament the belief was often "Be good
and be blessed; be bad and be cursed." This was why Job was
so perplexed by what was happening in his life. His repeated
question was, "What have I done that God has allowed this to
happen to me?" And to God directly, "Explain to me why I am
suffering like this even though I have honored all your laws!"

The belief was also carried over into the period of the New
Testament. In the Gospel of John, we see Jesus' disciples asking Him about the man who was blind from birth, "Who
sinned, this man or his parents, that he was born blind?" Jesus
shocked them by saying, "Neither." (See John 9:1–34.) The
cause of his suffering was neither personal nor generational.
Jesus gave a fascinating extended answer to His disciples on
the man's suffering, and it had nothing to do with either his
wickedness or someone else's.

In that context and in the larger one, Jesus explained that
though physical blindness is horrible, it is nowhere near as
horrible and debilitating as spiritual blindness. And then He
proceeded to heal the man, saying that the greater miracle was
to have the eyes of his understanding opened. The spiritual

suffering preceded the physical suffering and the physical healing was the lesser of the two miracles.

Then He ended His lesson with an indictment that shocked the legalists: Jesus said, "If you were blind, you would not be guilty of sin; but now that you claim you can see, your guilt remains" (John 9:41). Jesus lifted the entire question onto a different plane. They were much concerned about the man's physical blindness and totally oblivious to their own spiritual blindness.

As Worthy as Martyrdom

Islam truly does very little apologetic thinking on this subject. Their literature in this field is hardly abundant. On a popular level, Yasmin Mogahed has written a book called *Reclaim Your Heart*.[8] I have no doubt whatsoever that many high-level scholars will not take her seriously.

I said earlier that their thoughts on suffering come perilously close to the Buddhist and Hindu worldviews with dramatically different first principles and even more dramatically different results. Islam has often been described as a *pantheism of force*. It is a fact that in Islam the quid pro quo is so dominant that you are *compelled* to do things in a certain way or face destruction. I use the word *compelled* carefully. Muslims pride themselves in the Qur'anic verse "There is no compulsion in religion" (Qur'an 2:256).

But I ask you to take a look at any Islamic country. The subtle or overt threats or belittling a person is subjected to if he or she departs from the rules means that one is expected to comply. People do not have the freedom to *disobey* with impunity, and without that, there is no real religious or social freedom. It sounds very grandiose to say that there is no compulsion to believe, but the threat of punishment or torture where there is a violation is real and means that there *is* compulsion to believe.

What is meant by a *pantheism of force*? One term that Islamic scholars use for how to face suffering is the word *rida*— a technical term for being pleased and content. Note here the comments of sixth-century scholar al-Imam al-'Izz bin Abdi-s-Salam defining that term. Quoting from the Hadith, he says:

> *Rida* is the expansion of the heart to what has befallen it, its total acceptance of the divine decree and its not desiring to see it removed. Even though one may feel pain, *rida* lessens the pain because of the certainty and cognisance that has taken root in the heart. As the state of *rida* strengthens it is even possible that the person no longer feels the pain at all.[9]

Different from Buddhism, *rida* is not just indifference to pain or mere apathy. It is a cultivated positive well-being state of mind that transcends the outward circumstances; suffering is transformed from a negative to a positive. From this follows that sense of detachment and a gradual erasing of concern over any change in one's circumstances. Do you see the pantheistic nuances here? The goal is a near celebration without the emotion, even in the face of terrible pain and suffering.

Among Islamic writers the idea of detachment is used repeatedly. Here is Yasmin Mogahed. Notice her words:

Pain is a pointer to our attachments. That which makes us cry, that which causes us most pain is where our false attachments lie... We should only be attached to Allah... The pain creates a condition in our life... there is a divine formula to change it. God says: "Verily never will God change the condition of a people until they change what is within themselves." (Qur'an 13:11)[10]

Al-Imam al-'Izz bin Abdi-s-Salam says, "Any good thing that happens to you is from Allah. Any bad thing that happens to you comes from yourself."[11]

At a restaurant in Thailand owned by an Indian, I saw a wall plaque illustrating the essence of the Gita (a sacred text of Hinduism). It read "Whatever happened is good. Whatever is happening is also good. Whatever will happen, that will also be good." So it went on, ad nauseam. Needless to say, if I had walked out of that restaurant without paying my bill that would not have been good, and I would not be in good enough shape to be writing about it.

But these same responses to pain and suffering are intimated by *rida*. The follower of Allah is encouraged not just to be indifferent to pain but to experience sublime delight in suffering as evidence that as an obedient follower of Allah he cannot be hurt by it. It all becomes "good" for you.

Al-Imam al-'Izz bin Abdi-s-Salam actually takes it further. He moves from how to accept suffering, to how not to feel suffering, and finally to even applauding suffering, until the ultimate coward is the one who is not willing to be a martyr. Martyrdom becomes the sublimation of suffering. In one incredible passage he speaks of one lover saying to another,

> Were you to choose to afflict me with adversity
>   Truly delighted I would be that I crossed your mind.[12]

Elsewhere, he says:

> The believer is afflicted with tribulation to such an extent that he ends up walking on the earth with no trace of sin remaining on him . . . It is well known that everybody will die and the goal of the believer is that he be martyred in the cause of Allah for that is the most noble of deaths and the easiest.[13]

The idea of purging evil through suffering is pantheism in another form.

Yasmin Mogahed echoes the same thoughts. The formula for dealing with suffering is strictly a behavioral and belief code. She talks of how the love of *dunya* is at the root of all pain. (*Dunya* is the Arabic, Urdu, and Hindi word for "the world.")

Very cleverly she uses terms for which there are good and clear English equivalents, but by using different-sounding words, the intimation is that our own language is somehow transcended. This linguistic use is a strategic ploy in the mind of Eastern mysticism as well, trying to make their world seem different by introducing foreign-sounding words. In any language, "the world" means "the world" when the terms are clearly explained. *Dunya* is no different from Jesus asking

His disciples, "What good will it be for someone to gain the whole *world*, yet forfeit their soul?" (Matthew 16:26, emphasis added).

I do not need to introduce a foreign-sounding word to make it seem as though I'm saying something different and that the Westerner has no such equivalent. The meditation propagandists and those who insist that a language is sacred and that truth compromises translation are translating that very sacredness meaningfully, so it is assumed. Mogahed's book is replete with her native terminology as if to intimate that English simply does not have the same concept.

That aside, she goes on to say that the five pillars of Islam are a means to detachment. Then she adds this footnote: "Even our dress breeds detachment. The prophet tells us how to distinguish ourselves, to be different from the crowd, even in how we appear. By wearing your *hijab, kufi* or beard, you can't just blend in—even if you wanted to."[14] All these injunctions are important, she says, because a violation of these is at the root of pain.

Praying five times a day is another such injunction. By the way, Muhammad had first proposed praying fifty times a day. Then in a night journey he besought Moses to please bring some relief from such an obligation, so it was gradually reduced to praying just five times a day. Some teachings in Islam warn that if you miss just one such rotation, you are in danger of hellfire.

What is missing in Mogahed's treatment of the subject is fascinating. She has only brief chapters on love. Anyone reading her book with a clear mind will see what is absent—the bridge between the head and the heart. The love of God for you, the call to love God with your heart and mind, is present only as obedience to a legalistic measurement. The love of God and His reaching out for you is totally absent.

In fact, love as romance is almost mocked, as if romantic love is a childish thing to be engaged in. The notion of love in Islam is most instructive in that it is conspicuously absent. It is important for us to understand this.

Several passages speak of how Islam sees love. The following passage regards marriage:

> A man may question why he should show kindness and love to even a disrespectful wife. To answer this question, one only needs to look at the example of Omar Ibn ul-Khattab. When a man came to Omar (who was Khlifah at that time) to complain of his wife, he heard Omar's own wife yelling at him. While the man turned to leave, Omar called him back. The man told Omar that he had come to complain of the same problem that Omar himself had. To this Omar replied that his wife tolerated him, washed his clothes, cleaned his home, made him comfortable, and took care of his children. If she did all of this for him, how could he not tolerate her when she raised her voice? This story provides a beautiful example for all of us.[15]

The logical flow of this belief is evident:

If you experience pain, it is your fault.
So move to detachment, from being free from feeling pain to welcoming it.

Love as a concept is different, and the love of God becomes the demands of God.

Respect and love are often in vague confusion.

Suffering is atonement for one's wrongdoing.

There is total absence of grace and forgiveness; one always pays.

Religion is a means for paying for wrongdoing.

The renunciation of pleasure as sacrifice is the ultimate state of pleasure in material terms.

Martyrdom is the supreme triumph over pain.

Is it any surprise that one can inflict enormous pain on others in the name of martyrdom and consider life in paradise the just reward for that martyrdom? It is interesting that the infliction of pain is initially seen as a judgment for wrong, but is then strangely sublimated into becoming totally "pleasing" in one's own experience of pain.

Whatever else one wishes to make of all these thoughts, it is obvious that the very relationship between God and the individual person and the way suffering is seen and supposedly dealt with are vastly different in other belief systems from any Christian teaching.

As Complex as Our Differences

The net result of all this is that, East or West, the problem of pain and suffering is real and universal. The answers are sought from different directions because the ways of thinking differ on matters of pain and pleasure, among other things, and the presuppositions that are brought to the table are different.

In the West, the material nature of life is central;
in the East, the spiritual nature of life is central.

In the West, the body debates the reality of the soul;
in the East, the soul debates the reality of the body.

In the West, the soul becomes an illusion;
in the East, the body becomes an illusion.

In the West, the pursuit of control over pain is the responsibility of society and the effort is made to eliminate pain;
in the East, the pursuit of control over pain is the responsibility of the individual, and the effort is made to eliminate the personal cause of pain and suffering by exulting in the pain and changing it from a negative to a positive.

It does not seem accidental that the night Gautama Buddha left his palace to pursue an answer to pain and suffering was the very night his wife was giving birth to their son. In his quest to eliminate suffering, he actually walked out and left his wife alone in the throes of her pain. Contrast this with the God of the Bible, who came into this world Himself in the person of His Son to suffer on the cross, to embrace pain and suffering for the sake of humanity. Buddha walked away from his son and from pain. In Christianity, God is part and parcel of the solution. In nontheism or atheism, God has nothing to do with either the problem or the solution.

What difference does this starting point make? It is interesting that while for the Christian the suffering of the cross is at the heart of the gospel, Islam insists that Jesus didn't die on the cross. "To be humiliated at the hands of His creation is not a sign of power," they say. One can see that while the problem is admitted, the way of looking at suffering is vastly different.

So there we have it. The major religions of the world do address the questions of pain and suffering, but in a way that does not really answer them and really leaves unaddressed the reason for it all.

3. Naturalism: "No Meaning and Purpose"

All of this highlights the complexity of the problem of pain. There are at least three different aspects to it: (1) the metaphysical aspect—what is the source of suffering and pain, or the very concept of evil; (2) the physical aspect—natural disasters are not even thought of as being of humanity's making; and (3) the moral aspect—how can God justify the vastness of pain and still claim to be all-loving and all-powerful?

Behind this complexity lies the question of goodness and the ethical dilemma. But is there more to this? C. S. Lewis gives us a good analogy.[16] He states that when a ship is on the high seas, it must answer three questions. The first is how to keep from sinking—personal ethics; the second is how to keep from bumping into other ships—social ethics; and the third is the most important of all...to know why the ship is out on the high seas in the first place—what I call the essence of ethics. Why is there life at all?

When you differ on your answer to the third question, you differ in your starting point and your resulting implications.

For the atheist, this third question is the thorniest of all problems and is often just cavalierly answered: "There is no purpose to being out on this sea; it is just blind chance." "There is no reason for us being here, so we must make up our own reasons." "There is no real destiny for us, just the ultimate extinction of every individual." For the atheist, then, the most important of the three questions is moot, and the only ethics he or she can really talk about is personal and social ethics. Personal is one's individual choices. Social is cultural values dressed up as political theory.

This abandonment of purpose opens a floodgate of nonsense recategorized in empty terms. In one culture or religious belief, murder can be justified if it is branded "honor killing" or "blasphemy" against a prophet. In other cultures, right and wrong are categorized as "politically correct" or "politically incorrect," which moves one's choices entirely out of the realm of morality. (Those very terms, by the way, were coined during the days of cultural revolution in the West when politics was viewed with extreme skepticism, the days of the war in Vietnam when the political leadership was called into question. And yet now it is the basis of our determination of right and wrong.) So from honor killings in the East to political correctness in the West, we are all at sea without knowing why we boarded the ship in the first place.

I was at a university recently where there had been three suicides in the preceding few weeks. A lot of views and opinions from students were expressed in the university newspaper. One irate student castigated the authorities for dismissing such an important struggle as an issue of mental health: "That is not what this is always about," she stated. "I have no meaning and purpose in life, and the university is not helping me any." When an intelligent student in an Ivy League school is crying on the inside for help in finding meaning to life, it is time we realized that this is the same heart cry of millions.

And is that any wonder when the whole world is moving at such a high speed and no one really knows why we are here or where we are headed? It feels as if we are a ship out of control, careening toward disaster with no way to stop. With increased hope being placed in the sciences, the very purpose of life is going to be defined purely in biological and chemical terms. Science will determine that that's where it all began and that's where they pin their destination. Finding the purpose of life underlies all approaches to solving this mystery of evil and suffering.

As Definitive as Our Essence

At the end of the trail, it is left for death to define life. Even those who stoically face suffering at the end of their lives now are seeking to return in a different form that will end suffering, certainly a form that will end death. Recently I was reading about an Indian film producer who has made arrangements for his body to be kept frozen after he dies, in case science is able to bring him back to life in the future. He will be stored in a container in a vault in Arizona, at a facility called Alcor Life Extension Foundation.

He tries to live as healthfully as possible while he's here in this life, eating the right food, exercising, practicing yoga, and taking fish oil. "But when the inevitable [happens]," a team from Arizona "will place his body in ice-cold water and sustain his blood circulation and breathing with a heart-lung resuscitator. Gradually, his blood will then be drained to make way for an 'organ preservation solution' that will support life at low temperature. It's at this stage that his body will be packed in ice and air-dashed to Scottsdale."[17]

The corpses in this facility are then frozen in liquid nitrogen at minus 12 degrees Celsius until the day science has its own version of Easter for the masses. The article says that for such dead ones, they are "preserved in as pristine a form as possible," and "are spoken of as 'live-in customers.'"[18] They pay an initial fee and make arrangements for a monthly rental to be paid posthumously.

Remember the old joke of the wealthy man who asked to be buried in his Cadillac? A homeless onlooker whispered to another as they saw the car lowered into the grave, "Man! That's living!" It's not a joke anymore when a dead man can be called a "live-in customer"...except to the Alcor Life Extension Foundation, who can laugh all the way to the bank and change the P. T. Barnum conclusion that there's a sucker born every minute to "There's a sucker dying every minute." A full-body cryopreservation costs upward of $250,000. I would love to see someone write an article on what one can do with $250,000 to help the destitute live this life in dignity rather than using it to preserve corpses in the hope of another life.

I find it ironic that a man who resists putting chemicals into his body and eats only organic food will be chemically preserved in the hope of a future healthy life. Let us suppose that one such live-in customer dies at the age of ninety-five. And let us suppose that two hundred years from now science finds a way to bring him back to life.

What does a withered, ninety-five-year-old man, whose family chose not to be frozen and are now gone, do? Who reinitiates this person's status in life, seeing that he has reemerged two centuries later? For goodness' sake, even hairstyles are points of humor for the next generation. Imagine the jokes made about a ninety-five-year-old resuscitated body several generations from now. Will he be the dinosaur who is still kept in a confined space to be gawked at as someone from "once upon a time"? Will such a person be the museum species for the future? What will be the next step...a chemically induced, pain-free existence? Why would a person want to be resuscitated only to suffer the grief of lost relationships and to become a stranger at the hands of chemically altered practitioners?

And what will this all prove in the end? That it took intelligence to bring someone back to life...but that is the very starting point these live-in customers of the cryogenics facility do not wish to admit. Talk about being hoisted on their own petard! This sounds like the self-defeating argument of a person who tries to argue you into believing that argument doesn't work. He uses the means that he debunks to prove to you that it is effective after all.

If science did succeed in bringing the dead back to life, it would only prove that intellect was required to impart life to matter and not the other way around. Naturalism with its wonders seldom seems to ask itself the same questions it poses to those who believe that life has an ultimate cause and purpose.

So the complexity of the question lies not in the first two struggles of personal ethics and social ethics; rather, it lies in the third ethic—why are we here at all? Why do we seek to preserve that for which no purpose is known? If we preserve life because it has value, then we must ask where its value comes from.

You see how important purpose is to all these issues? Somebody else's purpose will govern our purpose if we ourselves do not define it clearly for now and the future. All personal and social ethics are subservient to a metanarrative for life itself. Who we are in essence governs why we are in existence. This question of purpose must be answered if we are to find significance in life and hope in death; from that follows the meaning of life even through suffering.

For the Muslim, submission is the supreme ethic from beginning to end until your endurance removes any present value from you as a person except as a ledger for good and bad. For the pantheist, total detachment from life and from relationships is the only way to avoid pain and suffering, similar to Islam but for a different reason. For the Muslim, it is because God is totally sovereign; for the pantheist, it is because the law of cause and effect is totally sovereign. For the naturalist, cause and effect is all material, and each of us just has to come in line with that. In all three there is, in the end, the loss of individual value and the stifling of the deepest longing of the human heart for love.

The definitions of human value and of love are either lost or obscured or trivialized. Without purpose, suffering is unexplainable. Without love, the meaning of life is unknowable. Each of these worldviews struggles to explain the tiny little purposes we all struggle with because they have no ultimate coherent purpose to offer. The most important elements that would complete the story are missing.

Worldviews Are Written

I began this chapter by acknowledging the connection between the music we sing and the arguments we make. Some years ago I was driving to a meeting and listening to some quite beautiful music on the radio that I did not recognize. But the song came to an end in shrill voices of screaming and fear. I reached to turn the volume down and wondered how that part of it could really be considered music.

Later I learned that the music was from the Broadway show of Andrew Lloyd Webber's *Phantom of the Opera*. When I finally watched the play for the first time and was able to track the story, I saw the beauty and the power and the reasoning behind the discord and screams in the music. It all fit into the picture of the deformed phantom, who loved Christine and taught her how to sing. Now, as he was losing her to the young, handsome Raoul, the phantom screamed his pain.

Yes, it is just a story. But it is the *story* that gives the chords and the discords their relative meaning. It is the *story* that provides the absolute. In fact, I remember asking the young woman who played Christine how it felt, night after night, to play the same role and sing the same music. Didn't it get tiresome? Her answer was fascinating. She said, "Two things make the difference. First, as soon as you hear the opening bars of the music you get into the role. Second, whether we realize it or not, how the audience engages with the story brings our own emotions into it." There you have it. The music sends the signal. The audience resonates with their response. The story takes over from the distractions of familiarity, and both the viewer and the actor are drawn into the narrative.

I have always maintained that the most gifted participant in the production of a movie is the writer of the screenplay, as it is the story that is supreme. But the role of the writer is seldom recognized because the actors have become the heroes. It is the same with a song. We admire the voice and the performer and lose sight of the one who wrote the words and the music.

When I was in graduate school, we used a massive Greek-English lexicon that we knew as A&G, the initials of the two authors that wrote it. My professor pointed out that this was a real tragedy because, in fact, they had not written it. They had just translated it from German into English. The man who wrote it was Walter Bauer. I heard it broke his heart that his life's work went unrecognized by the world of students and all the credit for his work went to others. I can truly understand such heartache as that.

Is there a story for life that explains our delights, our heart-aches, and our fears? We must understand the differences that worldviews bring to the discussion. For the atheist who sees no story other than one of his own making, the music and the emotion are nothing more than random dots along life's journey with no reason or meaning, and he ends up where he began...with nothing. The song of our life illustrates and beautifies the ultimate story, which must provide the back-drop from which to glean real meaning.

The heart responds to the imperatives of the mind. So what does one do with the pain and suffering that are part of the human experience...find various doors of rational escape? Let the heart feel the reason for which it beats. Let meaning and reason come together.

The pantheist is crushed by the moral law of cause and effect. The Muslim's only purpose in life is to fulfill that law as the cause for his or her effect. The skeptic cannot fully appreciate any music of life because the struggle for a moral law finds no definition. Hence, there is no moral cause or effect. She cannot escape the implications of her worldview and is trapped by her own questions.

Worldviews are written. When we view the world, we must ask, Who is the writer? Who is loving and creative enough to write meaning into even the most difficult parts of the story? Who would write Himself so deeply into our story that it would cost Him His very life? And if He has done so, will we lose sight of Him? Will we replace His name and one day forget it altogether? Or will we recognize His authorship and trust that an author who cares that much is an author who can write redemption into our unfinished story?

CHAPTER 6

A RESPONSE FROM MORALITY

Ravi Zacharias

We have evaluated the answers of the world's major religions to the question of suffering. We have also taken note of how the naturalist draws from the naturalistic framework to challenge the existence of God and the assertions of the Judeo-Christian worldview but isn't able to explain the evil and suffering that are realities in our world.

To attack another worldview without defending one's own worldview is not good reasoning, especially on a matter such as this. The naturalist has two responsibilities: first to defend his attack on the Judeo-Christian worldview; and, second, to justify his own explanation for pain and suffering. Let's examine the doors of escape the naturalist employs in trying to resolve the problem of evil and the reality of pain according to his worldview.

Door #1

This is the Evidential Argument from Evil. We looked at a portion of this in chapter 1. In this instance, evil as a category is used to argue against the existence of God. So by the naturalist's judgment, this is no longer a question for theism to answer; it is the justification for atheism. The deduction here is that whatever explanation there is or isn't, theism is a logical impossibility because of the presence of evil and suffering.

Notice how the tension is felt in trying to escape from having to defend their own position. J. L. Mackie posited that for him, the presence of evil made the defense of theism irrational. But this is the same Mackie who also said the following in trying to explain the conundrum of good:

> We might well argue...that objective, intrinsically prescriptive features, supervenient upon natural ones, constitute so odd a cluster of qualities and relations that they are most unlikely to have arisen in the ordinary course of events, without an all-powerful god to create them.[1]

In other words, objective moral values form such an extraordinary mix of features that the existence of God is the most likely explanation for them.

Obviously Mackie doesn't stop there, but before moving forward in his argument against God, he does grant that this is a real thorn for naturalism to explain. It is like an "on the one hand...but on the other hand" think-aloud monologue. On the one hand, yes, one can see that only the existence of God explains the objectivity in good. But on the other hand, evil is so obvious that it negates the possibility of God. For Mackie, the latter conundrum trumps the former, so, in his opinion, the case against God is settled. But the contradiction continues to haunt him.

The same dilemma is voiced with frustration by Canadian atheist Kai Nielsen:

> We have not been able to show that reason requires a moral point of view, or that all really rational persons unhoodwinked by myth or ideology, need not be individual egoists or classical amoralists. Reason doesn't decide here. The picture I have painted for you is not a pleasant one. Reflection on it depresses me...Pure practical reason, even with a good knowledge of the facts, will not take you to morality.[2]

Did you notice that line? "Pure practical reason, even with a good knowledge of the facts, will not take you to morality." What facts is he referencing?, one might ask. That it is wrong to torture babies? That intuitively we are repelled by genocide? That we cannot shake off "an ought" from "an is"? What are the facts he is talking about? Empirical facts, experiential facts, ethical self-evident norms? The impossibility of holding to the belief in naturalism that nothing is either good or bad and that reciprocal altruism brings about the well-being of all? The attempt to explain away moral reasoning as some bequest of evolutionary survival? What are these facts he is talking about?

The struggle is deep. So Mackie grants that an argument

can be made that the constituent factors defining intrinsic good and intrinsic evil form such an intuitively unexplainable pattern that only a theistic framework makes sense out of them. And Nielsen goes a step further when he admits that the categories of good and evil are actually rationally unsustainable by reason alone. The only conclusion that can be drawn is that there is no rationally compelling reason why we ought not to be individual egoists. This reality depresses him, Nielsen says…I can see why.

Is it not interesting that those who he says are "hoodwinked by myth or ideology" can give reasons for the categories of good and evil, and the "unhoodwinked" know that these categories cannot be supported by reason alone? The irony is that the rational "unhoodwinked" become depressed by this, and the irrational "hoodwinked" are at peace. So there goes the conclusion of this position bringing about "the well-being of all."

Enter Richard Dawkins, the master of belligerence. He says this:

> In a universe of blind physical forces and genetic replication, some people are going to get hurt, other people are going to get lucky, and you won't find any rhyme or reason in it, nor any justice. The universe we observe has precisely the properties we should expect if there is, at bottom, no design, no purpose, no evil and no good, nothing but blind pitiless indifference. DNA neither knows nor cares. DNA just is. And we dance to its music.[3]

I find this really fascinating. In a universe of blind chance, you would expect to see indifference to good and evil. I grant that. But one must ask, At what point did chance become design so that we *do* see something as good or evil? Is what we think we see not really what we think it is? Is the Hindu doctrine right, that it is all *maya*—an illusion, having at its core no qualitative difference? At what point does a DNA that "neither knows nor cares" become an arrangement that *does* know and care? How did the parts create so noble an embodiment of the whole that while in a description of who we are we are reduced, but in a prescription of what we think we are exalted? Does it really matter? Should it matter?

Let me give an example. The English alphabet has twenty-six letters. Suppose there were slots into which the letters of the alphabet could fall if tossed in the air, slots that could accommodate one, two, or twenty letters. Suppose further that we had designed millions of slots and that there were millions of pieces, each containing one of the twenty-six letters. Suppose you loaded a few dozen aircraft with these letters and let them fall from the air over these slots.

It is distinctly possible that you might retrieve from a number of these slots a word or words that had been formed by the falling letters. Since it is all by chance, in some slots there would be words, in other slots there would be non-words. And you might find that the same words had been formed in more than one slot. Let us say you had a billion years in which to keep doing this. Is there still any possibility that you could get an Oxford dictionary formed by such a process, words in sequence and alphabetical order? I wouldn't bet on it.

But that is precisely what Dawkins's argument compels us to believe; his is a designed argument against design, while the universe itself, according to him, has no design. He is the Oxford dictionary in a random universe.

If he is right and you would not expect to see design but randomness, at what point did design become supervenient over randomness? If nature had no prevision of the end, how is it that it blundered into design for moral reasoning while the process itself was amoral? How is it that over time, synchronically and diachronically, meaning with perfect time synchronicity and through the passage of time, we ended up with reasoning that brought morality into the logic of things? By naturalism's own admission, if you wind back the clock, you would never arrive at this design. It just happened.

In such a scenario are these categories of good and evil themselves not just tags we have given to something that is not essential but pragmatic? If survival is the ultimate ethic, what does that say about the numerous decisions we make that guarantee the nonsurvival of many, such as a parent sacrificing their life for the life of their child? Or a stranger dashing into oncoming traffic to rescue someone else?

Clearly, the ultimate ethic of survival is merely self-serving and nothing more than that, because it does not specify *who* should survive and to what end. Life truly becomes a pursuit of the unknown for no ultimate purpose but selfishly punctuated with tiny little arbitrary purposes. Everything will ever be in flux, and nothing will be of essential worth. If we are merely dancing to our DNA, some dancers are bound to step on others' toes, and it will hurt. Dawkins would say that it is better to be the one doing the hurting than the one being hurt because to hurt is not immoral, but to be hurt is to be at the wrong end of the pragmatic stick.

This is where the door to escape objective categories actually becomes a door to the denial of the obvious. Let me explain. Hobart Mowrer was a prominent psychologist who received his doctorate from the prestigious Johns Hopkins University. He went on to become a professor at Yale and at Harvard. As head of the American Psychological Association, he wrote an article in the *American Psychologist* titled "'Sin': The Lesser of Two Evils."

Before I go any further, think of the very title itself. Here is a psychologist with naturalistic assumptions wading his way through the existential struggles of moral definitions. And what was his conclusion?

> For several decades we psychologists looked upon the whole matter of sin and moral accountability as a great incubus and acclaimed our liberation from it as epoch-making. But at length we have discovered that to be "free" in this sense, i.e., to have the excuse of being "sick" rather than *sinful*, is to court the danger of also becoming *lost*...In becoming amoral, ethically neutral, and "free," we have cut the very roots of our being; lost our deepest sense of self-hood and identity; and, with neurotics themselves, find ourselves asking, Who *am* I? What is my *destiny*? What does living (existence) really *mean*?[4]

This is the deadly dilemma of the naturalist. By denying a transcendent basis for a definition of wrong, naturalists actually lose the definition of what "is." Forget about the "ought"; they cannot even understand the "is." The overt attack is on the "ought," but the real obliteration is of the "is." By decimating the "is," we do not know what it means "to be" or "not to be."

Dawkins very cleverly plays his word game again. How does he deal with this matter? His answer is that "a virus" has made its entry into the human software.[5] I suppose some viruses are just more virulent than others, to wit, Adolf Hitler and Joseph Stalin, responding to their viruses and dancing to their own DNA. And I also suppose that the Dawkinses of this world are the ones to expunge the virus.

Do you see what has happened? The mystery has encroached upon itself and devoured the questioner, who denies the moral law and, by inference, the moral lawgiver. The twin and painful ropes of determinism (where nature preconditions and determines all) and of evil and suffering ultimately strangle the one who kicks and screams against a moral order and purpose. It is a self-mutilation. The full force is felt when in denying the category of evil the naturalist actually posits the loss of self.

It is no wonder that satirists have called their bluff. G. K. Chesterton said it best:

> All denunciation implies a moral doctrine of some kind; and the modern revolutionist doubts not only the institution he denounces, but the doctrine by which he denounces it... In short, the modern revolutionist, being an infinite skeptic, is always engaged in undermining his own mines. In his book on politics he attacks men for trampling on morality; in his book on ethics he attacks morality for trampling on men. Therefore, the modern man in revolt becomes practically useless for all purposes

of revolt. By rebelling against everything he has lost his
right to rebel against anything.[6]

So by trying to escape from this door, the Evidential Argument from Evil, the naturalist finds himself in a quicksand
of his own worthlessness, unable to differentiate between any
worth.

The naturalist then tries a second door through which to
explain why theistic positions are not right, or certainly not
necessary, and why we can be good without God.

Door #2

In 1975, Harvard biologist Edward O. Wilson published his
work *Sociobiology*, in which he linked the physical with soci-
etal responsibility and, hence, coined the word used as the
book's title. Instead of the "bios" being the object of the study,
the "bios" now determined the study. Wilson makes this statement in his book: "Scientists and humanists should consider
together the possibility that the time has come for ethics to be
removed temporarily from the hands of the philosophers and
biologicized."[7]

So what started off as an explanation for good as individual
preservation became the preservation of progeny down the
road, then moved to genetic relatives and to reciprocal altruism
and now is, dramatically, "biologicized." Biology was wed to
sociology and metaphysics was supposedly rendered defunct.
The lines between disciplines became blurred, and a sleight of
hand moved self-determinism to determinism of self.

Metaphorically, the emperor still had no clothes, so a consensus was sought to somehow disavow philosophy while still making philosophical statements, to treat the body as matter and assert that matter really framed thought. Whatever else this proved, it demonstrated the heart-gripping nature of moral complexity.

Life is just too complex to make general statements on why I should abide by reciprocal altruism. What if my neighbor doesn't believe in it? What if my neighboring country doesn't believe in it? What if my spouse doesn't believe in it?

But let's go even further. There is a hierarchy to ethics that sometimes defies all of this. The love of a parent is often seen this way. How does one "biologicize" the choice of a mother in the peak of health giving up her life for a handicapped infant? How does one "biologicize" parents who drape themselves over a child to protect them from incoming mortar shells? How does one "biologicize" any self-sufficient being sacrificing themselves to protect those dependent on them?

The philosophical defense of naturalism was formerly the survival of the fittest. But we are talking of the survival of the weakest at the cost of the fittest. What law of evolution demands that? Suppose we can "biologicize" that by saying it is in the nature of things to sometimes make exceptions to the rule. What about a family that has been victimized by a brutal murder and looks squarely into the eyes of the murderer and says, "I forgive you"? What "biologicization" explains that? These are called supererogatory acts. In the evolutionary scheme, that category simply does not justify itself.

In his book *Emotional Intelligence*, Daniel Goleman tells the story of Gary and Mary Jane Chauncey, who lingered in the swirling waters of their compartment in a sinking Amtrak train, fighting off the current long enough to thrust their wheelchair-bound eleven-year-old daughter, Andrea, into the hands of rescuers.[8] Gary and Mary Jane perished in that accident, but they saved the life of their cerebral palsy–stricken daughter. That supererogatory act stirs the heart with noble example and reminds us that the "fittest" often do *not* survive in protecting the "most unfit" for preservation.

It is the very act of self-sacrifice that demonstrates that there is something more noble than mere survival. If Dawkins's presuppositions are correct, his book ought to be titled *The Selfish Genius* rather than *The Selfish Gene*. The Andrea Chaunceys of this world live at the bequest of a greater truth than "biologicization."

The big word *biologicization* actually shrinks the human story. The more the problem encroaches upon itself, the greater the loss of objective truth. So where does this lead us? In attempting to escape from the first door, branded the Evidential Argument, we arrive at the place where nothing is normative. In escaping through the second door of "biologicization," we arrive at the place where nothing is noble.

To be sure, let us clearly state what is not being said here by the theist. The theist is not denying that an atheist can be good. That would be preposterous and counter to fact. Atheists can be good and beneficent, and often are. But there is no *rationally compelling reason* for them to be good. "Reason doesn't decide here,"[9] said Nielsen.

We may as well call the categories yellow and blue rather than good and evil. These are colors with mere designations for visual recognition. But yellow is not any more good than blue is. The color scheme is descriptive for recognition and aesthetics, while good and evil are prescriptive for actions and imperatives for behavior. In fact, this was the mistake Bertrand Russell made in his famous debate with Frederick Copleston: When Russell was asked how he differentiated between good and bad, his answer was "[The same way] I distinguish between blue and yellow."

Copleston responded, "You distinguish blue and yellow by seeing them."

Russell agreed.

"So you distinguish good and bad by what faculty?" Copleston queried.

"By my feelings,"[10] replied Russell.

Well! A world's leading mathematician-philosopher differentiated between good and bad "by feeling"? As I have often said, in some cultures people love their neighbors; in others they eat them. Which feeling is yellow and which feeling is blue? And should we care?

Just one more thing. Good and evil go beyond mere laws of the land. It was at Nuremberg that the prosecuting attorneys finally asked in exasperation—when the defendants insisted on justifying their actions by saying they were acting according to the law of the land—"But gentlemen! Is there no law above our laws?"[11]

Moral reasoning *is* such a configuration that rises above mere preference and legality. One atheist may be a good person, but another atheist could be a bad person on the same grounds of reasoning. There is no rationally compelling basis for anyone to choose one action over the other.

That leaves the naturalist with one more door to try to

thrust open to escape the ramifications of his belief. But this time, rather than positing an option, he raises a question for the theist.

Door #3

From the Evidential Argument to the attempt to defend personal morality within their worldview, the escapist tries a final door. Now he asks why God could not have made humanity so that we would always choose good.

It is a fascinating question because it once again assumes a category (good) that a nontheistic framework actually cannot support. But be that as it may, apart from the obvious problem of making robots out of human beings, there is a larger question, and that is the question of love. Can one love without having the freedom to choose not to love? Determinism can condition compliance, but determinism cannot offer love. Even the existentialist Jean-Paul Sartre acknowledges that in *Being and Nothingness*:

> The man who wants to be loved does not desire the enslavement of the beloved. He is not bent on becoming the object of passion which flows forth mechanically. He does not want to possess an automaton, and if we want to humiliate him, we need only try to persuade him that the beloved's passion is the result of a psychological determinism. The lover will then feel that both his love and his being are cheapened... If the beloved is transformed into an automaton, the lover finds himself alone.[12]

Hobart Mowrer talked of the loss of the self. Jean-Paul Sartre took it further, to the loss of the significant other. When you are loved by someone who has been hardwired to love you, you find yourself alone. Why? Because the beloved doesn't love you by choice; the beloved loves by compulsion, which is not love. By definition the existentialist wishes to live for the now, with the will to choose and make his or her own meaning. If the possibility of love is denied within that volitional world, emptiness, aloneness, and desolation are the reaped consequences.

All of a sudden, from self-preservation and progeny-preservation we arrive at neither. My colleague Vince argued earlier that to ask for some conditions in our world to have been different is to end up asking for someone that is not you. Indeed, to make free choices without intrinsic freedom is to make something that is not human. In effect, the deed of mutilation is done. Naturalism kills both the general and the particular: the general care for our fellow human being and the particular love for our own offspring—the very two essentials that make our world possible.

This lamentable condition is where naturalism has brought us today. I remember some years ago, during the peak of his fame, reading an article about Elvis Presley in which the writer related an incident. He walked into Elvis's room while he was playing the piano and singing a hymn, almost as a plea. The biographer said to him, "How do you feel tonight, King?" Elvis answered in one word: "Alone."

How does one explain the "gods" of our time when they say they feel "alone"? We exalt them through the plasticity of our media and forget the solidity of the soul's hunger.

Every door of escape brings the haunting question of contradiction. As I said earlier, if one is willing to live with the contradictions of atheism, then why not give that benefit to God, too, and allow God to be contradictory and be all-loving while allowing pain? Why is it that *our* contradictions are not a problem, but God's contradictions defy reason?

The Trilemma Switches Sides

Is it not possible that the problem of evil is more explainable within the assertions of the Christian worldview than any other? What if I were to present the trilemma to J. L. Mackie this way, assuming his starting point:

> No God exists.
> Man is the source of all definitions of love.
> Good exists.

What an irrational set of propositions! Which of the premises will he deny? He will not deny the first. He cannot deny the next. He has to deny the last.

How does one even make the charge that God is not doing the loving thing by allowing pain and suffering without presupposing how love is defined? If man becomes the measure of all things, the next question is, Which man? Whose definition supersedes all others? J. L. Mackie's? Dawkins's? Or do we invoke a selective sovereignty over the right to define?

Explaining the absoluteness of evil within the theistic paradigm is far more rational than trying to explain the absoluteness of good within the atheistic paradigm. So is the next step to deny good? Raising the trilemma and positioning one's own trilemma does not make one irrational and the other soundly coherent. Good and evil do form the opposite poles of our human struggle, and to deny either is to deny an inescapable reality.

The assumption that God is contradictory because he allows evil and suffering to be part of our experience is false, and living with such a belief is devastating. Once again, the musicians take us to the land of reality as the atheistic philosophers took us into the land of unreality. Once again, their bluff is called because the heart cannot accept what they have tried so hard to espouse.

In 1991, the Geto Boys released a song titled "Mind of a Lunatic" that celebrated the most horrendous evils one could imagine. It sold a million copies within days of its release, demonstrating without any doubt that the doors of escape proposed by naturalism bring society into a land of the monstrous. The songs of a nation reveal more about how we're thinking and feeling than do the philosophers and lawmakers. Life without moral reasoning makes all definitions, in the words of the Geto Boys, "helter-skelter."

The poet Steve Turner reveals the same:

If chance be
the Father of all flesh,
disaster is his rainbow in the sky,
and when you hear

state of emergency

sniper kills ten
troops on rampage
whites go looting
bomb blasts school

it is but the sound of man
worshipping his maker.[13]

Putting it plainly, naturalism—with its critiques of theism and its attempted defense of moral reasoning—falls short on both counts.

So where do we go for an answer? Pantheism is trapped in its own definitions of karma, with existence being timeless but individuals being finite. Each life rises without knowing how much it owes and when it will all be paid up, and even those who supposedly have paid up still have desires that were the cause of suffering in the first place. So the ideal is violated by choice, when choice itself is the problem.

Atheism starts off with a question that posits certain categories, and then is ultimately forced to actually deny such categories. Atheistic thinking is also trapped in the vise of determinism but somehow rises above it when it argues for morals, believing passionately that humans are free but all the while discrediting the reasoning behind what makes us free.

In short, pantheism and atheism end up in the same predicament: Both are playing God. The only difference is that one denies matter, while the other denies the spirit. In recognizing the place of the Creator and His purpose, the Christian faith affirms the reality of both the physical body and the soul.

This is a key priority. As George MacDonald said, "Never

tell a child you *have* a soul. Teach him, you *are* a soul; you have a body."[14] In the recognition of that, pain and suffering are explained, and the greater needs of the soul and its expressions are given their rightful place. Since the spiritual and the physical are kept in balance, the two great truths emerge—the need for redemptive and sustaining grace and the supremacy of love. These truths surface right from the beginning and never cease to be needs.

May I present two simple illustrations? A dear friend who works in our ministry had a surprise pregnancy when she was around forty. The doctor gave her some tests and concluded that the risk that the baby was abnormal was too great and strongly recommended an abortion. She said she would not go that route and would have the baby. The doctor was so firm in his insistence that she abort the baby that she didn't feel comfortable any longer as his patient and found another doctor.

The baby was born in due time, not only as healthy as any child but in fact he is far superior in intelligence to his peers and always at the top of his class. He is fluent in English and Spanish and has now asked to learn Mandarin.

When he was younger he looked at his mother one day, all dressed up for an evening out with her husband, and said to his father, "Daddy, isn't Mommy looking so pretty tonight?" Like a typical male in his middle years, his father took a quick glance at his wife and replied, "Yes." Andreas reprimanded his father, "No, no, no, Daddy! That's not how you say it. She's not just a friend. She's your *wife*! Look at her again and say, 'Patricia, you are beautiful!'"

Here's the amazing extension to that story. The children's clinic where Patricia takes Andreas for medical checkups and care is in the same building as the office of the doctor who wished to abort him. On one occasion she tried to introduce Andreas to the doctor, but he refused to meet with them. The hubris of playing God ultimately makes it almost impossible to accept the evidence that shows you to have been so wrong, in this case so wrong that he would have destroyed a life with great potential for splendor and hope.

Turning a blind eye to reality will not eliminate it but will only heighten our indictment. So we swing from the Scylla of freezing the dead in the hope that we might resuscitate them at some future time to the Charybdis of killing the living in the hope that we will never have to see them.

The Bible makes an extraordinary claim in Psalm 8:

> O Lord, our Lord,
> how majestic is your name in all the earth!
> You have set your glory above the heavens.
> Out of the mouth of babes and infants,
> you have established strength because of your foes.
> (verses 1–2 ESV)

The psalmist talks of the glory of creation in the most exalted terms and then of the glory of praise from infants and young children. How on earth can an infant even utter praise?

The baby's very existence reveals the cardinal excellencies of faith, hope, and love. Just think of that. When Paul said that there abide these three things, faith, hope, and love, and that the greatest of these is love, he identified the three great excellencies of which both children and adults are capable (see 2 Corinthians 13:13). A child lives with incredible faith. When he or she cries, it is in the hope that the cry is heard. When arms envelop that little one, love is expressed. All of these concepts are best represented in a child, even before he or she is capable of expressing them.

Though love is the central feature, our offspring still endure pain. I was raised in an atypical, upper-middle-class family. In India, there are different mind-sets even at the same socio-economic level. In an arranged marriage, my dad was quite anglicized; my mother was not. My family descended from the highest caste of the Hindu priesthood, but several generations ago, a conversion from Hinduism to the Christian faith took place. It is a long, fascinating story. However, as generations descended, that very faith became nominal and nothing more than family tradition.

In my upbringing, I was subjected to what today would without a doubt be considered severe child abuse. I was terrified of my father. I was never belligerent toward him, but I wasn't walking in the academic discipline that he wanted. It was very ironic that he loved sports but never came to see me play. I loved sports, too, and I was good at them. I honestly think he was just a busy man. The seduction of power in India is great, as it is now more subtly than overtly in the West.

Having suffered much at my father's hands, we had no relationship. It was my mother who carried me through. But in my own dramatic conversion in my teens after having attempted suicide, my life turned around. My father watched that progression with shock and admiration. Sadly, I lost my mother in my twenties, a hard and painful loss to this day.

My dad lived with remorse for those lost years after his own life was transformed when he, too, trusted Christ as his Savior. Years later when I received my first honorary doctorate, he sat in the front row and his face told the story. My father was only sixty-seven when he died; I was in my early thirties.

This is what I want to say: Two things happened in my dad's later years that I still find emotionally very moving. In my twenties, before I flew to Cambodia to speak, my dad handed me a letter and asked me to wait to read it until I reached Phnom Penh. I could hardly wait.

When I arrived I was taken to a missionary's home to stay. There were blackouts throughout the city because of the terrible war within the land, so I used a flashlight and sat up in my small bed to read my dad's letter. Never in my entire life would I have expected to read the regret, remorse, and vulnerability with which he wrote, basically asking for forgiveness and speaking with pride in his son, the son he had been sure would never make anything of himself.

I have four siblings; I am the second born. All admit that for some reason I took the brunt of my dad's vicious temper. Yet when he needed a ride to the hospital for elective bypass heart surgery, he asked me to take him. We talked alone, something that had never happened before, as it had been bred in me to look for any reason not to be alone with him.

He seemed to sense, for some reason, that he may not come through the surgery. We put it down to his melodramatic personality. But he wanted to get his house in order. I knew how much I loved my dad even though the memories of my childhood and youth with him were painful. I believe he really thought he was doing what was right, though he was so sadly wrong. That day was a reminder to me that we all have our failings, however well-intentioned. None of us are free from that.

I prayed with him, bid him good-bye for the moment, and promised I would be there for his return after surgery. Except...except, he never came through the surgery. He struggled for days, perhaps able to hear us even though he could not communicate, and within the week he passed away.

As I write now, I am the same age as he was when he died, more than three decades ago. And when we parted, everything I wanted restored had been restored. The pain I experienced has given me a tender heart for the weak and exploited of this world. The failures I knew have given me hope that lives can change and the assurance that the Grand Weaver does weave a beautiful design, albeit sometimes with strange threads. God is able to help us conquer *through* suffering, not just in spite of it.

Whether it is in the life of a little boy who almost never had the opportunity to live or a young man who didn't want to live, the story of love and forgiveness wins the greatest battle of all in the soul. The body of pain will one day be cast aside. The soul that enjoys God's love and forgiveness will live forever.

Love and forgiveness. Remember those two terms. That is the story of the gospel. No other faith or philosophy tells that story.

CHAPTER 7

A RESPONSE OF HOPE

Vince Vitale

Hope Against Suffering

For one of my birthdays when I was a little kid—I must have been about eight—I asked my dad to build me steps up this massive tree in our backyard. That year he built a few wooden steps for me to climb, and then we made a deal that every year on my birthday we would add a couple of steps to the ladder.

And I thought it was so cool. I remember thinking that many years from then I'd be able to climb up hundreds of feet and look out over the entire neighborhood.

Of course, it never occurred to me how dangerous that would be or the suffering it could cause. As a child I had these great dreams for the things I would do and the person I would become. Nothing seemed out of reach! And it just never occurred to me that suffering could get in the way.

I can remember as a kid believing that I could fly. And I'm not talking about in an airplane. I can actually remember going into the backyard and believing that if I closed my eyes and tried hard enough, I might actually open them to find myself hovering off the ground.

I can also remember thinking I would never die. I would try to imagine myself coming to the end of my life, and I just couldn't conceive of it. I remember believing I would fall in perfect love, a love that would never fade. I remember believing I would become a professional athlete, go on awesome adventures, change the world, make a real difference. And it just never occurred to me that suffering could shatter these hopes.

Does this sound familiar? Or if not specifically my weird dreams, what were your childhood dreams? What were your expectations for your life as a child? What were they ten years ago? How about five years ago? What are they today? How have they changed?

Many people start out with extraordinary dreams, but by the time they are adults they have ceased to dream like children. We learn to set our expectations low, to bring our hopes and dreams down closer to where we already are.

And in a lot of ways this makes perfect sense. We don't want to be dreamers, hopeless romantics, naive idealists. We were ignorant when we were children. Now we understand the harsh realities of our world. Now we understand how often expectations are unmet, and the hurt that brings. Now we've experienced failure. We've had relationships end badly; we've had parents divorce; we've had loved ones die; we've lost friends to suicide.

In turns out that what's outside of us isn't what we had dreamed of, and what's inside of us isn't what we had dreamed of either.

What's Outside

I had this innate sense as a child that the world was going to be kind to me, that every year things were going to get better and better, and I was going to climb higher and higher. And why not? Every year I was getting faster. Every year I was getting stronger. Every year I was getting smarter.

But somehow, without my even realizing it, childhood turned into young adulthood, and I got busy just trying to keep up with the pressures of life and doing all of the things that everyone told me I was supposed to be doing, and I completely forgot about those steps in the backyard.

And years later I remember looking back at them, and they were weak and rotted. I tried to have a climb for old time's sake, but they wouldn't hold my weight anymore. I couldn't even climb back to the step I had gotten to as an eight-year-old.

We want to believe that the world is on our side, that the world is going to be kind to us and give us opportunities to climb higher and higher each year. We try to convince ourselves with hopeful phrases:

The world is your oyster.

The sky is the limit.

The only thing to fear is fear itself.

You can do anything if you just put your mind to it.

Things can only get better.

Such nice phrases. But here's the thing: They're all lies! Every one of them! They are simply false. There are so many things to fear in this world other than fear itself—disease, abuse, betrayal, accidents, poverty, failure…For many millions of people in this world, poverty is the limit, or slavery is the limit, or depression is the limit, and experience suggests that things won't get better.

As I write this I'm in my early thirties, and already so much of what I looked forward to as a child, so many of those steps I had dreamed of, are rotten and lost for good. I'm never going to look better; I'm never going to run faster. I'm never going to be stronger. My body already has titanium screws holding together its left shoulder and knee and torn ligaments in its ankles, and it's only going to get weaker and weaker until eventually my body stops working altogether.

Sure, I have relationships that I find value in—my marriage, for instance. But how much confidence can I really have that my marriage is going to have a happy ending when the divorce rate is about 50 percent?

And even if Jo and I do stay together, even then our marriage isn't going to have a happy ending, because it's going to end when one of us dies. It's amazing how little many people think and talk about death. Perhaps it's because we don't want to face the reality of it. As Aldous Huxley put it, "[T]he knowledge that every ambition is doomed to frustration at the hands of a skeleton [has] never prevented the majority of human beings from behaving as though death were no more than an unfounded rumour."[1]

We would think about death all the time if we had a life-threatening disease. But isn't that exactly what we all have? Our bodies are all slowly dying. And that's only if we happen to live long lives. One unintentional yank of the steering wheel the next time we're driving, and we're done. Forgetting to look before crossing the street, just once, and that could be it. That's how fragile we are.

I guess we can hope for a peaceful and painless death in old age, but the truth is there's no such thing. We hear of a man dying painlessly in his sleep, but what we don't hear about is the wife who finds her husband the next morning. Someone is going to be in pain—maybe us as we die, maybe our loved ones as they watch us die. Either way, there is no such thing as a desirable death.

I know this is all a bit heavy, and I'm not trying to depress anyone. I'm just trying to be honest about the fact that there is no reason to think the world out there is going to be kind to us.

What's Inside

But what about what's *inside* of us? Maybe that's where our hope should come from. Perhaps we can feel good about the fact that regardless of how difficult our circumstances may get, we can be good people and take pride in that.

But I think if we're honest about what's in our hearts, we have to admit that we have as much to be ashamed of as we do to be proud of. At least I have to admit that. I have to admit that Jesus was right when He said, "What comes out of a person is what defiles them. For it is from within, out of a person's heart, that evil thoughts come" (Mark 7:20–21).

I personally had a very hard time coming to accept the reality about the sin in my life. Our tendency can be to judge ourselves in relation to one another, and we can always find a neighbor or someone on the six o'clock news who, by comparison, makes us look pretty good. But in my most honest moments I knew that wasn't the case.

I remember even as a teenager I knew I wasn't living the life that I was meant to live. But I told myself, "I'm young. Everyone does stupid stuff when they're young. One day I'll decide it's time to live 'the good life,' and then I'll just 'flip the switch,' and I'll be a good man. Then I'll be the man I know deep down I ought to be."

And then I tried flipping that switch, and I fell flat on my face. And I tried flipping it again, and again I failed, and in the process I hurt myself and many of the people I love most.

So much of our suffering takes root not only because we are living in a world that often seems against us, but because we are not the people we know deep down we were created to be. Life is not headed for a happy ending, not only because of the harsh world outside, but also—if we're honest with ourselves—because of what's inside.

And so what happens? We stop having great expectations for life. We stop dreaming like we did as children. We expect less; we hope for less; we settle for less. Maybe a great novel or an epic film takes us back to our childhood dreams momentarily, but then we remember—only in the movies do dreams come true.

Redemption

Here's the point I really want to make: Jesus Christ is in the business of redeeming expectations. He's in the business of reviving hope. In their magnitude and beauty, His expectations for our lives have much more in common with our childhood idealism than with our adult realism; they look much more like what we once dreamed of than like what we now settle for.

And here's why. Because when you choose to live with Christ, He begins to transform you from the *inside out*. He begins to transform what's within, and that begins to transform our experience of what's without.

Internal Redemption

Before I was a Christian, I can remember being at a high school party and getting the brilliant idea to run around my friend's house in just my boxers, with my T-shirt pulled up over my head. (At the time this seemed like such a good plan.) Now what everyone *conveniently* forgot to tell me was that my friend's parents were putting an inground pool in the backyard, and so far all they had done was dig a massive mud pit in the ground.

Yup! I ran right into it. It was just like one of those cartoons when someone runs off a cliff and the legs keep running, and then—bam!—straight down into the mud.

When you are drunk on alcohol, you find yourself doing things that otherwise you would never do. You're more confident. You're funnier. You're a much better dancer (or so you think).

There's a passage in the Bible that says we should not get drunk on wine, but instead be filled with the Spirit of God (Ephesians 5:18). You see, this drunken desire to go beyond oneself, to transcend oneself, to do adventurous and heroic things, is in its undistorted form a good desire and from God. It's connected to that childhood desire for greatness that I was talking about earlier.

But drunkenness or drugs or promiscuous sex or pornography or power trips or the newest technological toy, or whatever it is that we get our highs from, is just a terribly cheap imitation of the real thing.

When you decide to be a Christian, when you invite God into your life, the Bible says that His Spirit comes to live inside of you (Romans 8:9–11)—a spirit so powerful as to have raised Jesus from the dead. And it is just remarkable to experience the Holy Spirit living inside you and empowering you to be more and more the person that you long to be and that you were created to be.

When you are filled with the Spirit of God, you again find yourself acting in ways that you know you otherwise couldn't, or wouldn't. You find yourself with an inexplicable love for the person you used to find most annoying, with courage and confidence in the situations in which you know you always buckle, with patience and gentleness in the situations that usually make you angry and violent, with joy where there was sadness, with a peaceful night's sleep where there was worry and anxiety.

I used to play soccer with a guy who said: "You become a Christian so that you can live the life."

Becoming a Christian is not just a matter of believing something different, but of stepping into an empowering relationship with Jesus that will give you the strength to live the life you were made for.

I have no doubt that without God in my life, I would be an unfaithful husband headed for a destroyed marriage. Before I was a Christian, I cheated on practically every girl I dated; I would spend my money on no one but myself without giving a thought to the fact that others don't even have enough food to eat; I was someone who would rather give a bloody nose than take one for someone else.

But from the time that I said "yes" to God, He began to

transform my heart, so that I could start to become a faithful friend, a faithful son, a faithful husband, and so that Jo and I could have confidence in our marriage.

God will not coerce you; He will not change you against your will. But as a Christian, you freely ask God to give you the strength to follow Jesus, to follow the life that He lived—a life devoted to seeing others through suffering and to loving them sacrificially.

When you tell God that following Him is the desire of your heart, you find yourself with a strength that is beyond your own, a strength to be more of the person you were created to be for the people you care about most, to be that person you dreamed about being as a child. Søren Kierkegaard put apt words to the experience: "Now, by the help of God, I shall become myself."[2]

External Redemption

And when God begins to transform what's within us, this begins to transform our experience of the world outside of us as well. Suffering remains, but now it is experienced in the context of a relationship with a God who is stronger than the suffering.

I often wish I could describe to people in full the experience of being a Christian. I think to myself, *If others could just experience living with Christ from the inside, there is nothing they would desire more.*

One way I can begin to describe my experience of life with Christ is like this: Have you ever had the experience of feeling that you were doing just what you were made to do? For me it was sports. Those rare moments on the field when

172 • WHY SUFFERING?

everything clicked. Maybe for you it's music or art or some-thing else—when every moment is filled with significance, purpose, meaning. Anxieties fade, and you know that you are just where you are supposed to be, doing just what you are supposed to be doing. Or maybe for you it's not so much an activity but a place—that one place in the world where you feel completely like yourself, where you are perfectly at home.

In Christianity, I found that rather than these experiences being the exception, they became the norm. Jesus invites that peace and contentment to be a part of our everyday—that sense of purpose, that sense of significance, that sense of home.

This is absolutely not because things always go my way. Many Christians experience just as much or even more suffer-ing once they begin to follow Jesus. Rather, it's because I know there is a God who loves me just the same whether things go my way or not—the same on my best day and on my very worst day—and because His Spirit is not only in church buildings and on mountaintops but has come to live within me, and remains with me every second of every day, no matter where I am or what I am doing. The apostle Paul put it stronger still: "I am convinced that neither death nor life, neither angels nor demons, neither the present nor the future, nor any powers, neither height nor depth, nor anything else in all creation, will be able to separate us from the love of God that is in Christ Jesus our Lord" (Romans 8:38–39).

How Big Is Your God?

Your God will be as big as your dreams and expectations. If your expectations are low enough, you can get away with being your own god. I did for a long time. If your expectation is to be well-connected and to run in the right circles, the city can be your god. If it's to be rich, money can be your god. If it's immediate pleasure, sex can be your god. But I think deep down many of us sense that we were made for more than this.

The Bible says that "[God] has set eternity in the human heart" (Ecclesiastes 3:11). He has set in our hearts that child-like desire to be part of something extraordinary. And the invitation to become a Christian is an invitation to raise expectations, to reclaim childlike dreams.

The world tells us that we should set only the goals and have only the expectations that are within reach. The Christian claim is exactly the opposite! God should set our goals and expectations, and these can be way beyond our own reach because there is a God who has really conquered sin and death, "who is able to do immeasurably more than all we ask or imagine, according to his power that is at work within us" (Ephesians 3:20). And when we say "yes" to Him, we step into a new life with Him where "nothing will be impossible with God" (Luke 1:37 NRSV).

Jesus said it this way: "I have come that they may have life, and have it to the full" (John 10:10).

Ask a Christian if life has been easy, and she'll say, "No." Ask a Christian if his life has turned out the way he thought it would, and he'll say, "Definitely not." But ask a Christian if her life has exceeded expectations, and a likely response will be "Absolutely." She'll tell you that even amid the suffering, life has been deeper and more meaningful, more filled with purpose and awe and a sense of home, than she ever could have imagined.

And this is only the beginning, because if God can redeem my heart within, and if He can redeem my experience of the world without, then I have every reason to trust that one day He will redeem all of creation.[3]

Hope Amid Suffering

Choosing to live with Christ is choosing to take a stand against suffering; God begins to heal the brokenness within us and He begins to transform our experience of a broken world. But on this side of eternity, suffering remains very real, and too often very severe.

Something that has surprised me as my colleagues and I have spoken around the world is that the problem of evil—raised invariably in the West—is rarely raised in the parts of the world where people appear to be suffering most. All around the world, counterintuitively, we find that often the people who have suffered most severely somehow have the greatest confidence in the goodness of God.

I've spent a lot of time reflecting on why this might be the case, and I don't have a complete answer, but perhaps it is in part because there are certain things about God's goodness and about God's response to suffering that can be known only by inviting God into our suffering and experiencing Him in the midst of it.

In philosophy, this type of knowledge is referred to as non-propositional knowledge, which is to say that it can't be fully conveyed by words, by writing it down in a book to be read. This is different than just saying it is a mystery. Non-propositional knowledge can be known, but only by experiencing it firsthand.

And actually, quite a lot of our knowledge is like this. Jo and I recently spent time in Florence and had the privilege of viewing Michelangelo's *David*. To be honest, it didn't feel like much of a privilege as we stood in line in the rain for two hours waiting to get in. Nor did it feel like a privilege when Jo and I "discussed" our difference of opinion about whether it was worth continuing to get rained on to see something that we had both already seen countless times in photographs and on television.

We stayed. And when we saw the *David*—in person, up close—we were so grateful that we did. Only then did we *know* what all the fuss was about. We knew something by experiencing that piece of artwork firsthand that had not been conveyed to us—that *could not* be conveyed to us—by postcards or documentaries.

Likewise, there were things that Jo and I learned by directly experiencing Florence as a city that we could not have learned from a distance. We stayed with two dear friends who had already expressed to us as best they could what they love about Florence and its culture. But no matter how well they described Florence to us in conversation or in e-mails, there is a knowledge of that place that we could access only by visiting it. Just telling us couldn't do it. Perhaps reading a good novel set in Florence would have helped. But, really, for us to properly grasp what our friends knew and loved, we needed to book a flight and spend time there.

Much of our knowledge is knowledge gained by experience, above and beyond anything that can be known by description or argumentation. And this is even more frequently the case when we start talking about the knowledge relevant to relationships.

For instance, I know my wife's face. But no matter how many pages you gave me, and no matter how much detail I included, I could never express to you the fullness of that knowledge in writing. A spreadsheet with the exact dimensions of Jo's face still wouldn't tell you what I know. There would always be more that I know when I actually look at her. That knowledge I can share with you only by introducing you to her.

I could say the same of simply knowing Jo—knowing who she is. I could tell you about Jo all day long, but still I wouldn't come close to expressing to you the fullness of my knowledge of who she is. That depth of knowledge can be acquired only through the interactions of intimate relationship.

Not all knowledge is propositional knowledge, the sort you can give an argument for on paper. Some knowledge can be gained only in person, and in relationship.

This is true of much of our everyday knowledge. Perhaps it is also true of knowledge of God, and in particular knowledge of God's goodness in and response to suffering. Maybe much of *that* knowledge, as well, cannot be known by philosophical argumentation, but only by inviting God into our suffering— by voicing our frustration to Him during it, by praying to Him through it, by experiencing it together in relationship.

A medical doctor recently wrote to me and put it this way:

It seems to me that when we speak in a theoretical sense about terrible suffering of cancer patients or orphans, we miss a good deal of the picture. When people actually engage with and enter into the experiences of real, live cancer patients, or go to experience life at an actual orphanage, people tend to come away from those experiences strengthened in their faith, not weakened. It's often right where suffering happens that we personally experience God.[4]

What we learn about God in those experiences has something to do with the fact that He has suffered with us. I have already suggested that there is a bond and a depth of relationship that is possible only between people who have shared the worst—those who have laid in the trenches together, those who have walked each other through the wreckage of a natural disaster, those who have held hands at a deathbed. By suffering with us and sending His Spirit to live with us through all that we suffer, God ensures that the strongest possible bond we can experience and the deepest possible relationship we can enter into are both with Him.

What we learn when we endure suffering together with God also has something to do with how different the experience of suffering is when it is not suffered alone. To me, one of the most depressing images in Scripture is that when Jesus' suffering was at its worst, all of His friends "deserted him and fled" (Matthew 26:56). Suffering's greatest cruelty is its isolation, isolation that robs us of hope. But the experience of suffering is radically different when someone who loves you is right there with you every step of the way. Something about suffering *together* gives reason to hope.

And when you are in Christ, you never have to go looking for someone who understands your suffering. You never have to go looking for someone who cares. That someone is always with you, even within you. For we do not have a God who is distant—high in the sky when we die—but One who has known sorrow (Mark 14:34); One who has wept (John 11:35); and One who "is not far from any one of us" (Acts 17:27).

I can glance in these ways toward something of what can be known about the problem of evil by inviting God into our experience of suffering. But precisely because much of this knowledge is non-propositional, I'm unable to say much more. The meaning in suffering and in God's response to suffering is largely to be found not in theorizing but in the life of faith, as we identify with the God who suffers with us and for us, and with His people, who know what it is to live by His side.

Some of the most important knowledge in life—whether of Florence, or of a friend, or of God—cannot be grasped from a distance. I think we are inclined to miss this in part because the philosophers in us typically prefer to see our arguments laid out neatly and conclusively on a page. But upon reflection, it is unsurprising that there is something to be known about the way God is present in suffering and working amid suffering that can be known only by seeking Him in our suffering. We have seen that much relational knowledge is non-propositional, and the Christian response to suffering is primarily not a response of theory but a response of a Person and a response of relationship.

Perhaps this is why so many come to trust God after a period of suffering. Perhaps this is why those who have been through suffering often emerge more rather than less confident in God's goodness. Those same people sometimes have trouble fully expressing *why* they are so confident in God despite the terrible suffering they have been through. We may be tempted to brand such people as deluded or as holding on to Christianity merely as a psychological crutch. Such people are irrational, we might be inclined to think, if they profess belief in the goodness of God even though they can't give their full reasons for that belief when challenged.

But if this is how we think, we are guilty of bad philosophy. People can be perfectly rational even when they cannot perfectly defend the rationality of their beliefs. Why? Because there is something they know through suffering in union with God that it's not possible to know through arguments. And if that is the case—if some of the reasons for trusting God amid suffering can be accessed only from the inside—then the strongest response to the problem of suffering may often be for the Christian to invite the skeptic to join him in responding to real life suffering by turning to God.

I suspect this is one of the reasons why the Bible is so narrative. As a great novel set in Florence can *almost* take you there, many of the stories recorded in the Bible invite you into the experience of suffering with God and of knowing God.

One of those who suffers most severely in the Bible is Job. And his question, expressed tirelessly and through tears, is the question of this book: "Why?" No simple answer to Job's question is recorded in the text, and yet at the end of the narrative Job encounters God—"My ears had heard of you but now my eyes have seen you" (Job 42:5). And in that seeing, Job knows a peace that none of his arguing and theorizing could provide.

Christians don't just claim to know this or that theory about why God allows suffering. They claim to know God Himself— *who* He is—and that knowledge is a deeper and more intimate knowledge than anything that can be expressed in words alone. This is not a response to the problem of evil of the kind philosophers tend to seek; it is not a response that I or anyone else can put to you in paragraphs. But it is a response I can invite you into.

If we are serious about evaluating the problem of evil based on all of the relevant evidence, we first need to ask whether we have invited God into our suffering, and whether we are willing to. Perhaps you began reading this book thinking that if there is a satisfactory response to the problem of evil, then you will begin praying to God and asking Him to be involved in your life. The argument of this section suggests that this may be backward, that one of the strongest responses to the problem of evil can be known only by first being willing to invite God into your experience of suffering.

This invitation can be extended even before you know whether God exists. I remember in my own life extending this invitation with the silent words *God, I don't know if You are there, but if You are, I want to know about it, and I want You to be with me through what I am dealing with right now.*

For many of us, if we're honest with ourselves, we know God about as intimately as we desire Him. If we desire Him enough to seek not only answers to questions but His face, then in knowing His face we may find the very answers we seek. And we should not be surprised that a God who values relationship above all would see to it that some of the most essential things to know about Him are knowable only by taking a step toward relationship with Him.

Granted, there are times when suffering can descend on us like a heavy fog, and we need someone to remind us that

God is not far and to tell us in which direction to step. I wrote one of the last sections of this book on a flight from London to New York. As I came through security at Heathrow Airport, I had about an hour until my departure, and I had it in mind to find a quiet spot and make a start on the writing I had planned.

As I began to walk toward the departure gates, a small sign for the "Multi-Faith Prayer Room" caught my eye, and instantaneously—though I have never before had an urge to visit an airport prayer room—I felt this conviction that there was someone in that room whom I was supposed to talk with. It was as if someone had just told me, "There is someone waiting to speak with you there," even though I had not audibly heard those words.

I did an about-face and walked a good distance away from my departure gate to the arrivals terminal where the prayer room was located. When I walked in, there was one man in the room, sitting in a corner on the floor. He appeared to be about my age. When he saw me looking around the prayer room, he asked, "Are you religious?" We began speaking about what it means to be religious, and he soon shared with me that he was going through the worst suffering of his life.

Mohammed fought back tears as he shared about what no one would ever want to go through. He expressed that he never talks about such things with anyone, but that he just needed to get it out. He told me that he used to pray five times a day, but that now the suffering is too much; he opens his mouth to pray to God and nothing comes out. Finally, Mohammed challenged me, "If God exists, why is there so much suffering? And where is He amidst it all?"

Now I understood why we were supposed to meet. I told Mohammed that the one person of whom he finally asked "Why suffering?" was currently writing a book by that very title, and in fact was walking in the opposite direction toward the departure gates when God turned him around and led him to this specific room to share that God does care and that He is present.

Sometimes God is most present when our suffering can make Him seem most absent. Sometimes when we are in the fog and are unable to see much on our own, we need people by our side to show us where they see God in our lives. Sometimes we mistake God's respectfulness for absence. Understandably there are times when we want God to be more obvious. But God desires to reveal Himself clearly to those who desire Him, without revealing Himself forcibly to those who do not.[5] He wants us to follow Him not because He is overpowering, but because we trust Him.

Mohammed was in a place where he couldn't see God. But God was with him. Mohammed was in a place of tough questions. God crossed his path with someone who could appreciate those questions. Mohammed was in a place where he couldn't pray. God provided someone to pray with him.

As we parted, Mohammed and I shared an extended hug that spoke deep understanding, deep appreciation, and deep friendship. We had spoken and prayed together at length about what it is to believe in, and to love, and to live with a God who knows suffering Himself, and who is never absent in our suffering. "He is not far from any one of us" (Acts 17:27), even if sometimes we need others to step with us in the direction that leads to relationship with Him.

Hope Beyond Suffering

Nothing brings greater hope in the Christian faith than the fact that the relationship God desires with each one of us is not fleeting or for a limited time only. Because Jesus endured suffering to the end, and yet by His resurrection proved that death is not the end, our friendship with God can be for all eternity.

My cousin Charles died a few years ago. He went to dinner with my aunt Regina, and he started choking on a piece of food, and a minute later he stopped breathing. That was it. Without God to turn to, what could be more senseless? Without God to turn to, everything and everyone is headed toward death and injustice.

But as a Christian, I can't tell you how thankful I am to know, with great confidence, that Charles is with the One who chose him and loved him even before the creation of the world, with the One who was willing to suffer alongside him, and that I will see Charles again. I will see him in a place where the Bible says "[God] will wipe every tear from [our] eyes," where there will be "no more death or mourning or crying or pain" (Revelation 21:4).

If this suffering-free world is possible, we might wonder why God didn't just create us in it from the start. No doubt heaven has some amazing advantages over our current world—utter intimacy with God and with others, the end of all suffering. But there is also value to be found in our current world. I don't believe that God desires suffering, but by allowing suffering in this world, God makes possible certain good

184 • WHY SUFFERING?

things that otherwise would not be possible. As I argued in chapter 3, one of the good things made possible is our existence as the particular individuals we are. Among the other goods are courage in the face of danger, standing against injustice, showing compassion and empathy, the freedom to love, sacrificing one's own good for the good of someone else. These are among the goods that we value most highly, and all of them are by their very nature responses to and therefore dependent on the possibility of suffering.

I find it interesting to note that when *we* create worlds—movie worlds, for instance—we, too, tend not to create utopias with no possibility of suffering. Without the possibility of serious suffering, there would be no Frodo, no Forrest Gump, no Superman. The difference, someone might point out, is that in these movie worlds things work out well in the end. But of course, according to the Christian story, that will also be the case with our world.

There are definitely wonderful heavenly goods that are not possible in a broken world. But there are also some goods that are possible only in a world that includes at least the potential for suffering. If God values all of these goods, then it would not be surprising for Him to allow us to exist at one time in a world that includes the possibility of suffering, and then at another time in a redeemed world where suffering will be forever defeated. And if suffering pains God as it would any loving parent, then it also would not be surprising if God set things up so that the portion of our lives that includes suffering could be much shorter than the portion that does not. In both respects, this is precisely what Christianity claims.

As I mentioned earlier, when my mom saw me running

home from neighborhood football with tears streaming down my face, all she wanted was to keep her child safe—to take me inside and protect me. That's what she *wanted* to do. But she knew that if I was to become the man I needed to be, she couldn't just miraculously take away the problem every time I started to cry. And so she sent me back out into that game.

But she also stayed on the front porch, and she kept her eyes on me. It mattered to her that however badly the game went, when it was over she *could* wrap me up in her arms and take me inside and bandage my wounds; ultimately she *would* be able to protect me.

I think this matters to God, too. This book has suggested that there are numerous reasons relevant to why God might allow suffering. And here we can add the following to those reasons: God knows that one day soon He will take us out of suffering, He knows that what He can take us to will be a state of great joy, and He knows that from the perspective of eternity the proportion of our lives that we will spend amid suffering will be remembered as a "flicker" at the very outset of our existence.[6]

A Matter of Perspective

Imagine aliens who somehow managed to tap into a video feed from earth, but all they could see was the hospital delivery room when I was being born. And they watched as the doctors forcefully told my mom to do things that made her scream in pain. And then when she could take no more, the doctors got out a knife and cut right into her stomach. They took me out—blood everywhere—and even though my mom was reaching out for me and screaming for me, they immediately rushed me away from her.

What would the aliens think? If all the aliens saw were the first few moments of life, they might think the doctors were utterly evil. They might also conclude that bringing a child into this world is a terrible crime. Only from a fuller perspective would they be able to see that the doctors actually cared for my mother extremely well, and in fact saved my life. Only from a fuller perspective would they be able to understand why many of us are in fact grateful to our parents for having given us life.[7]

The problem of evil is in part a question about how much of reality we currently see. In the Christian understanding of reality, what we currently see is only the first few moments of life—literally just the birthing process of human history. If we assume these first moments are all there is to life, then we may very well doubt the goodness of the Creator. But this doubt will be overcome when our view is widened and becomes the view from eternity.

How decisively this doubt will be overcome depends on how good God's offer of eternal life turns out to be. Many of those who seem to know God best suspect that our tendency is to vastly underestimate just how great eternal life with God can be.

I was studying the Old Testament book of Job recently, and one of the commentators picked up on a detail that I had never noticed. At the beginning of the book, Job loses everything—his wealth, his livestock, his family. At the end of the book, we are told that God gives back to Job a double portion of everything that had been lost—twice as many animals, twice as much wealth. But Job gets back only the same number of children. Job lost ten children, and he's given back ten children at the end of the book.

Why is that?

Perhaps because Job still had his original ten children. Perhaps they were not permanently lost. Job was not with them for a time, but maybe he will be reunited with them in heaven for all time.[8]

And this is not just an ancient story but a very present reality for so many who trust in Christ. Close friends of mine and Jo's found out two weeks ago that they had miscarried. It was a very hard time, filled with grief and with worry about the operation our friend had to undergo due to complications. Here is the message we received from them just after they returned home from the hospital:

> We just got back from the hospital. It was a long day. The surgery seems to have gone fairly well, although there was a lot of bleeding (Erin lost fourteen times the normal amount). As a result she will be pretty out of it over the next little while as she recovers...
>
> We named the baby Hope.
>
> When Erin suggested the name, it just seemed right. Because of our faith, death is not the end. We have Hope. Hope for a later time of being a family together with this little one, and hope that death will not reign in our family... there will be more little feet to come.

Some of us have lost people very close to us. Some of us have hoped for things in this life that have not come to pass. In the life to come, God can give back to us so much of what has been lost. He can fulfill so many of the dreams that have been shattered.

We will always come up short if we attempt to find the full explanation for suffering in this life alone. This life accounts for only the smallest fraction of our lives. We are going to live forever. And even though right now we live in a harsh broken world, Jesus promises that one day "everyone who calls on [Him]" will live in a world that will be good to us (Romans 10:13; Acts 2:21; Joel 2:32).

"Do You Believe This?"

When I was a kid, I used to think I would never die. Jesus says I had it right.

Billy Graham once said, "Someday you will read or hear that Billy Graham is dead. Don't you believe a word of it! I shall be more alive than I am now. I will just have changed my address. I will have gone into the presence of God."[9] What a blessing to be able to speak those words with confidence, to know in your heart that death is an "unfounded rumour," that you're not just headed for death, but that every day you are headed for greater and greater life.

With God, our childhood optimism was correct. We *do* have reason to hope, to hope amid the brokenness of this world and to hope beyond that brokenness as well. Perfect love *is* real; we *can* live forever; there *is* no limit; things *can* get better.

When things get worse before they get better, God is with us. And as we look to the future we can trust in the words of Jesus: "I am the resurrection and the life. The one who believes in me will live, even though they die; and whoever lives by believing in me will never die. Do you believe this?" (John 11:25–26).

Three weeks ago I shared these words with the father of my

oldest friend. I grew up right next door to them. In fact, it was on their front lawn that I started crying during that neighborhood football game many years ago. As I write this, my friend Chris's father—Joe—is suffering from a brain tumor, and the doctors have given him two days to a week left to live.

When I walked in to see him, I didn't know if he would want to talk about his approaching death. Joe had always been strong and capable. He had a voice so deep that no matter what he was speaking about, it resounded with confidence and authority, leaving little room for vulnerability.

But as soon as Joe saw me he said, "Hey, Vince. Good, I'm glad you're here. I told Chris I wanted to talk to you." Joe went on to tell me that although he had always been confident that God exists in some way, he was finding himself increasingly scared about what comes next.

As we spoke, what became clear to me was that Joe's understanding of the central message of Christianity—of what it takes to be right with God—was that you should try to do more good than bad in your life, and then just hope that in the end your good deeds will outweigh your bad deeds. If they do, something wonderful awaits. But if they don't, you're in trouble. And as Joe reflected back over his life, he recognized that if that was the case, then he—like the rest of us—had reason to fear.

Never was I so incredibly thankful to be sitting before someone as a Christian. Other ways of seeing the world would have had nothing to say. As an atheist, I would have had to say there is no hope at all beyond the grave. If I adhered to almost any other religion, I would have had to tell Joe that he was basically right and had every reason to fear what was next.

Only as a Christian could I explain to Joe for the first time that while Christianity *does* say that God wants us to do good, that is *not* what makes us right with God. I was able to share with him that the message of Christianity is that what makes us right with God has nothing to do with anything we do or ever could do, but rather with what Jesus has already done—once, and in full, and for all. I explained that if we trust in Jesus Christ, we no longer need to fear judgment, because Jesus has already taken the judgment for everything we have ever done or will ever do wrong.

I explained this at length, and when I asked Joe if this made sense, he responded—in classic New Jersey fashion—"That's a hell of a realization." Emphatically he said it again, "That's a hell of a realization," and then continued, "Sixty-nine years and I never thought of that. I thought Christianity was one thing, but it was something else entirely." There was an extended pause, and then Joe said, "You know, Vince, you spend your whole life trying to make up for your [mess] ups, but this finally explains how we can deal with guilt."

I asked Joe if he wanted to pray with me to accept this gift from God—to trust in Christ's sacrifice and not in our own works—and he said he did, and with great conviction he thrust out his arm to me. We clasped hands, and we wept, and we prayed, and as we finished praying he exclaimed a loud "Amen."

Joe asked me if my wife, Jo, knew this great truth about Christianity as well. I said that she did, and he said, "It must be a happy life." And then, after a thoughtful pause, "Now I'm actually looking forward to what's next."

When Joe's family saw him the next day and asked how he was, for the first time in a long time he responded, "Wonderful." The transformation in him was so visible that his family called me immediately and wanted to know every word that I had shared with him.

Life after death, on its own, does not bring hope. Only grace brings hope. I know of no grace as extravagant as the grace of Jesus Christ. And as grace upon grace—because Jesus has already done *everything* necessary for us to be right with God—this greatest of all hopes can be received with a simple heartfelt prayer.

One of the arguments of this book has been that the rationality of Christian faith is not undermined by the existence of evil and suffering. But the challenge suffering poses to belief in God is not the *only* problem of suffering. There's also the problem of how we're going to *deal* with suffering, and that's a problem for every one of us, regardless of what we do or do not believe about God.

Some think the problem of suffering should push us away from God. For me, it's precisely because I feel the problem of suffering so severely that I am led to trust a God who can do something about it.

Each one of us is going to deal with significant suffering in our lives. And, one day, each of us is going to have to deal with the reality of death. That could be sixty years from now; that could be choking on a bite of chicken at dinner tonight. When suffering comes, when death comes, who will bear it with us? Who will see us through it?

Jesus will, if we ask Him to. He won't force Himself into our lives. But if we invite Him, then we will never be alone in our suffering, and we can trust that we will spend eternity in a place where suffering will be no more.

Chapter 8

God's Manifold Responses

Vince Vitale

We hope you have found the previous chapters helpful. One of our aims has been to show that there is not just one or two but many Christian responses to the challenge "Why suffering?" We haven't tried to present every important response to this question, but we have tried to present a variety of responses that we believe make sense and make a difference.

How should we judge the success of these responses? This depends crucially on two additional questions:

Should we expect a fully satisfying response?
Do *more* responses make for a *better* response?

Reason Not to Expect a Reason

Should we expect to find a fully satisfying answer to the question of why God allows suffering? Good reasoning suggests perhaps not.

When my brother Jay takes his cat Sonny to the vet, Sonny doesn't understand why Jay needs to allow her to suffer the pain of a needle. And when Jay sits Sonny down on the couch and tries to explain to her that this suffering is important so that she won't get a terrible disease, Jay doesn't get very far.

This is not because of some lack of ability on my brother's part. It's not because he's not a good enough communicator. Sonny simply isn't the sort of being that can comprehend why Jay does many of the things he does. Sonny's ability to understand is limited with respect to the being that is caring for her.

You can see the analogy. If God exists, He is infinite in every respect; He is even further beyond us in intelligence and understanding than my brother is beyond his cat.

Our ways are higher than Sonny's ways. Why, then, should we be surprised when God's ways are higher than our ways? Why should we be surprised if fully understanding God's ways requires capacities that—at least for now—finite creatures like us do not possess?

A child's struggle to understand his parents' reasoning suggests another analogy. The decision to move from one city to another may be experienced by a five-year-old as the absolute worst suffering that could ever occur. In the moment, the child might be absolutely certain that all happiness is behind him, that his parents hate him, and that for all practical purposes his life is over.

And yet even such outrage on the part of a child does not mean that the child's parents are wrong to make the move, and it does not mean that they don't love him. In moving to a different city, the parents may be doing what is best for the family; they may even be doing what is best for their child, despite the fact that the child is unable to understand or accept that.

These are trying times for a family. But years later, as children mature, they often can look back and see the good reasons their parents had for making decisions that, at the time, seemed like the end of the world. With time, the child might even come to no longer wish away the move.

The gap in understanding between human parents and a five-year-old child is great. The gap between God and us is much greater still. Should we be surprised, then, if God's decisions rely on understanding that presently we cannot grasp?

Infants recognize the goods of food and warmth, but not much else. Children begin to grasp the goods of protection and of friendship. If we mature well, adulthood brings a greater appreciation of morality, of beauty, and of justice. It is often the matriarchs and patriarchs of our families who seem to have a still greater perspective on what is good and true, a perspective that sees far beyond their own interests to the lasting love and loyalty that can bless a community down through the generations.

With each stage of maturity—if we mature well—we are able to appreciate good things that we were blind to when we were younger. And along with this we are able to appreciate what it sometimes takes to realize these goods—the commitment, the sacrifice, the suffering.

We all agree about this. We all agree that greater maturity allows for greater understanding of what is good, of what is bad, and of how sometimes the possibility of the bad is the only way to secure the best of the good. If we all affirm this reasoning in general, to then deny it just because the being in question is God would be pure bias.

When we move to a new city, we trust that as hard as it is for our children, they will understand in time, once they are more mature. By the very same reasoning we can trust that a perfectly mature being would be in a position to understand all goods—including goods that currently we cannot even fathom—and also to understand the logical connections between those goods and the possibilities of suffering that they entail.

Moreover, as good parents look forward to the day when their children are old enough to understand, so, too, God looks forward to, and indeed promises, such a day:

> When I was a child, I talked like a child, I thought like a child, I reasoned like a child. When I became a man, I put the ways of childhood behind me. For now we see only a reflection as in a mirror; then we shall see face to face. Now I know in part; then I shall know fully, even as I am fully known. (1 Corinthians 13:11–12)

Here's the main point; one of the assumptions smuggled into the thought that suffering disproves the existence of God is this:

> If God does have good reasons for allowing the suffering that He allows, *we* should know what those reasons are.

But why think that? God might have many reasons for allowing suffering. And we shouldn't be at all taken aback if we aren't able to grasp them in full.

What most people find when they reflect deeply about suffering is that it is not that difficult to think of plausible reasons for why God might have allowed *some* of the suffering they've been through. But other instances of suffering defy understanding, and, even after sustained reflection, no plausible explanation presents itself.

If that's what we find after serious reflection, we shouldn't be surprised. If God is as awe-inspiring as Christians claim He is, that's exactly what we should expect to find. That's what we should expect when considering the ways of a God who does desire for us to know Him, but who is too big for us to fully appreciate all of His reasons.

We see what we should expect to see if God does exist. How, then, can what we see be strong evidence that God does not exist? It cannot be.

If I asked you whether there is a spider in the room you are sitting in right now (or in your general vicinity if you are outside), you would be thinking irrationally if you told me that you are confident there is not a spider because you can't see one.

Why irrationally? Because even if there is a spider in the room, there is no reason you should expect to see it. *Sometimes* we see spiders, but they are not easy to spot in a sizable room, and many times we are blissfully unaware of their company.

It's likely that things would look exactly the same to you even if there were a spider in the room. Not seeing a spider is just what you should expect if a spider *is* in the vicinity, and therefore not seeing a spider cannot be strong reason to believe a spider is not around. Sorry if I just ruined your sleep!

With respect to God's reasons as well, many times we do

see them, but many times they are difficult for us to see from our limited, finite perspective. And as deeply frustrating as that can be, it is just what good reasoning suggests we should expect.

Tim Keller puts it very well:

With time and perspective most of us can see good reasons for at least *some* of the tragedy and pain that occurs in life. Why couldn't it be possible that, from God's vantage point, there are good reasons for all of them?

If you have a God great and transcendent enough to be mad at because he hasn't stopped evil and suffering in the world, then you have (at the same moment) a God great and transcendent enough to have good reasons for allowing it to continue that you can't know. Indeed, you can't have it both ways.[1]

Over the last thirty-five years, this general form of response to the problem of suffering has produced one of the most prolific discussions in all of professional philosophy of religion, and it has been powerfully defended by some of the best philosophers of our time. In the ongoing philosophical debate, this response goes by the technical name "Skeptical Theism."[2]

But it's not a new idea. We find it in the Bible in several places, for instance in Paul's letter to the Romans:

Oh, the depth of the riches of the wisdom and knowledge of God! How unsearchable are his judgments, and his paths beyond tracing out! (11:33–34)

And before that we find it in the book of Isaiah:

"For my thoughts are not your thoughts,
neither are your ways my ways,"
declares the Lord.
"As the heavens are higher than the earth,
so are my ways higher than your ways
and my thoughts than your thoughts." (55:8–9)

It should give us serious pause if we assume that God can have good reasons for something only if *we* know what those reasons are. What does that assumption assume about who we are? The Bible puts the question this way:

Who has known the mind of the Lord so as to instruct him? (1 Corinthians 2:16)[3]

It takes an extraordinary amount of confidence in one's intellectual abilities to claim, "I know the sort of world God should have created." Isn't that a claim to know as much as God Himself?

Personally, I find myself wanting to be very cautious when I start making claims about what sort of world God should have created. My experience of universe-creation is zero, so I just don't know that much about what universe-creation takes or about how all of the good possibilities and all of the bad possibilities hang together.

As we seek to understand why God would allow suffering, it's important to set the bar for success at the appropriate height—the height suggested by good reasoning.

When we do, quite contrary to feeling at a loss when confronted with the objection from suffering, I find myself surprised and encouraged at how many things we can say. Given the transcendence of God and the finitude of ourselves, what's remarkable is how many of God's reasons we *can* understand, at least in part.

Though perhaps this, too, should be unsurprising, because while the Christian God is indeed infinitely beyond us, He has also lowered Himself, making every effort and every sacrifice in order to reveal His love to us in the person of Jesus Christ:

> Who, being in very nature God, did not consider equality with God something to be used to his own advantage; rather, he made himself nothing by taking the very nature of a servant, being made in human likeness.
>
> And being found in appearance as a man, he humbled himself by becoming obedient to death—even death on a cross! (Philippians 2:6–8)

Many Reasons, Many Responses

Ravi and I have suggested there are many reasons for thinking that the existence of suffering does not negate the existence of a loving and powerful God:

> We claimed that God's gift of freedom itself is not evil but rather the precondition of love, and that our abuse of that gift is the cause of so much of the evil and suffering around us.

We suggested that one of the reasons God values this world is His love for you—as the unique individual that you are—and we suggested that we should be slow to impugn God for creating a world that included the possibility of suffering when the creation of a different world would have meant our probable nonexistence.

We concluded that if God has willingly suffered death on the cross, He has made such an extravagant display of His love for us that it is rational to trust Him, even when we lack full understanding.

We highlighted that the strength of any explanation depends on the plausibility of alternative explanations, and we commended to you the distinctiveness of the Christian explanation of suffering, in both the seriousness with which it takes suffering and the richness of its response to suffering.

We explained that the moral outrage at suffering that often motivates the problem of evil finds its justification in the very God that it seeks to dismiss.

We suggested that a good creator might allow suffering if He also provided the power to stand against it. Our consistent experience is that the Christian God has provided such a power.

We observed that for many people, God's presence and goodness are more rather than less real to them in times of suffering, and we suggested an explanation for this in a relational knowledge of God that is less like reasoning about someone and more like seeing someone with one's own eyes. This, too, is reason to trust God amid suffering.

We think that the afterlife matters. It matters to a parent's decision to allow a child to suffer whether ultimately the parent could take the child out of that suffering and defeat it. God can do just that.

We argued that—given our finitude—far from being disappointed by this array of responses, we should be surprised that there is so much to say.

There is no need to choose between these reasons; none of them deny any of the others. Personally, I accept every one of them as having some significant role to play in a successful response to the objection from suffering.

These reasons for denying that suffering undermines the goodness of God also raised some worthwhile questions:

Have we considered the objection from evil and suffering not against God, but against ourselves? And how will we respond to that objection?

Could God have wronged you by creating a world in which you came to exist and are offered eternal life, rather than creating a different world in which you never would have lived?

If creating people in a world in which they will suffer is in principle immoral, then is it wrong for human parents to have a baby?

Could someone who would rather die than see you in suffering, sin, or shame really be someone who is against you?

Who tramples reason, the person who says there is a good God or the person who says there is not even good or evil?

Is there another way of viewing reality that responds to suffering with the grace, compassion, and courage of Jesus Christ?

Is the loving parent the one who never allows the possibility of suffering or the one who ensures that there is reason to hope even in suffering, and reason to hope that suffering will one day be overcome?

Is it at all surprising if God has reasons that are presently beyond our ability to see or comprehend?

One thing that listing all of these questions in succession highlights to me is that there was never a point at which God was not responding to suffering in some significant way. From all eternity He has been the standard of goodness that opposes the evil of suffering. In creating He chose, by grace, to love human beings despite their vulnerability to suffering. When humanity fell into sin, God would not reject us. By becoming a man, He suffered with us. At the cross, He displayed the limitlessness of His love for us. He sent His Spirit so we would know His presence amid suffering and have the power to stand up under it. He sends His followers to every corner of the earth, to share with all people everywhere that suffering need not be their end. And in the end, He will ensure that, if we trust Him, suffering will be no more. At every point in salvation history, within every major doctrine of the Christian faith, there is a substantial divine response to suffering.

It is in God's manifold responses to suffering that so much of what we love and care about finds meaning. Here is one final thought experiment that helps me to understand why, when all of the reasons are considered together, a good God might make the difficult decision to allow suffering.

Think for a minute of one of the greatest lives ever lived. It might be the life of someone you've known personally or of a historical figure you've studied.

Consider this life in detail. Think of the person's character and how it was formed through his or her free choices. Think of the person's moral convictions and the principles that he or she lived by. Think of the various cultures and subcultures that framed what she valued and what she experienced. Think of the person's relationships. Think of her great triumphs, her sacrifices, her steadfastness for what is good and true. Take a bit of time to reflect on these things.

Now try to subtract from that person's life all of the suffering—the suffering that shaped the culture and family she was born into, the suffering that formed her character and convictions, the suffering of her loved ones, the suffering she fought against.

What happened?

All of a sudden those lives don't look anything like the great lives that we were initially so inclined to celebrate. Could we even sensibly speak of them as the same people?

We say we want a world that will never include the possibility of suffering, but do we understand what we ask for?

Without the possibility of suffering, practically every great true story in history would be false. No one would ever have made a significant sacrifice for anyone else. No great moments of forgiveness and reconciliation. No opportunities to stand for justice against injustice. No compassion (because nothing to be compassionate about); no courage (because no dangerous situations requiring courage); no heroes. No such thing as "lay[ing] down one's life for one's friends" (John 15:13).

Love itself would be called into question. God could miraculously prevent our actions from ever causing one another to suffer. But if no matter how you spoke to me it sounded good, if no matter how you touched me it felt good, then your words and your touch wouldn't communicate love. There would be no way for me to tell that they were expressions of love rather than of hate.[4]

Is it so obvious that the world I have just described would be a more desirable world? Is it so obvious that God would create that world rather than our own?

Many of the greatest actions and affections—the things most worth celebrating—can occur only in response to the possibility of deeply regrettable outcomes. Wouldn't a God of justice create a world that could seek justice? Would a God of love create a world that could love? Wouldn't a good God create a world in which the person whose life you celebrate most could have lived that praiseworthy life?

It is far easier to wish vaguely for a better creation than to imagine concretely what one would be like. But criticism without alternative is empty. And so the question arises: If not this world, what sort of world should God have created? I find that the longer you think about that question, the harder it is to give a compelling answer.

Often we wish we could just delete the possibility of suffering from this world without changing anything else. But that won't work. We fail to recognize how much good would be lost in losing the *possibility* of the bad.

It is true, I believe, that one day God will bring the suffering of this world to an end. But on that day the celebration will not be that there was never the possibility of the bad. It will be far greater than that. It will be that the possibility of evil has been triumphed over, forever defeated by the necessity of the good—God Himself.

Strength in Numbers: Is More Better?

There are a great variety of reasons to deny that suffering disproves God's existence. But is more better? Do many reasons make for a better case overall?

Well, sometimes. Let's say you know a couple who have decided to try to have a child, and you ask them, "Why?" If they respond that they are looking for someone to clean their house cheaply in a few years' time, you would quickly and rightly tell them that's a despicable reason to have a child. But what if they told you they had other reasons as well? What if they told you that they are hoping to have a child because they want to make their other children jealous, and because they want other people to think well of them, and because they'll get a significant tax break?

Now they've given you four reasons instead of one, but it's made no difference to their overall justification for having a child. No matter how many unreasonable reasons you stack on top of one another, the conclusion will still be unreasonable. If the value of each reason given is zero, $0 + 0 + 0 + 0$ will still equal 0.

But the result is different if each of multiple reasons has

something to be said for it. If the couple told you they want to have a child because they have a desire to love a child, you might be satisfied. But you might ask them to say more about their reasons. In that case, they might add that they think they can provide well for a child, that they think bringing another child into their family would be a blessing to their other children, and that as a couple they have had some success in raising happy children in the past.

In this case, each of their reasons is a decent reason for having a child; each has something to be said for it. This allows the reasons to reinforce one another. Even the person who is suspicious of the couple's reasons after hearing only one of them might nevertheless judge that their decision to have a child is clearly justified when the reasons are considered altogether. When individual reasons are *good* reasons—when they each have some value on their own—then more reasons do generally make for a better overall reason.

Throughout the pages of this book, Ravi and I have offered about ten primary reasons for why God might allow suffering. What this analogy suggests is that even if you question whether any of those reasons are sufficient to justify God's allowance of suffering on their own, when considered cumulatively they may nevertheless be more than sufficient, and therefore point strongly to the goodness and trustworthiness of God.

More reasons make for a stronger response to the objection from suffering in a second way as well.

Say a jury has one piece of evidence that casts doubt on what they at first assumed would be a guilty verdict. Will that be enough for them to change their minds and rule "not guilty"? It might not be. Perhaps a witness *thinks* she saw the defendant in another part of town when the crime was committed, but her eyesight isn't the greatest and she admits she can't be *sure* that it was in fact the defendant whom she saw. This *might* be enough to raise "reasonable doubt," but it might not be. The jury might remain convinced of the defendant's guilt.

But what if the defense was able to present not one but ten pieces of evidence, all pointing to the defendant's innocence? What if ten people independently thought they saw the defendant across town at the time of the crime? If ten people, from ten different perspectives, all thought they saw the defendant on the other side of town, then the only rational conclusion would be that he was on the other side of town. And note that this would remain the case even if each of the ten witnesses had some doubt about what he or she saw. Even so, the chance of all ten of them seeming to have seen the same thing is so improbable otherwise that it overwhelmingly confirms that the defendant was in fact across town at the time of the crime.

Or, if we want to vary the reasons implying the defendant's innocence, what if in addition to a witness who thought she saw the defendant across town, there was another witness who thought she heard his voice across town, another who saw his car across town, another who was having a relaxed phone conversation with the defendant at the time of the crime, another who testified that the defendant could not be out to hurt the victim because he had willingly risked his life for the victim just prior to the crime's occurrence, another who thought she saw someone else commit the crime, another who showed that the defendant stood to lose a great deal as a result of the crime and that a second suspect had a much

stronger motivation to commit the crime, another who produced a restaurant receipt suggesting that the defendant was
out to dinner at the time of the crime, another who confirmed
that the defendant passed a polygraph test shortly after the
crime, and a final expert witness who testified that hair and
skin samples found at the scene of the crime did not match the
defendant?

If all ten of these witnesses were called to the stand, the
jury would undoubtedly acquit. And, again, note that this
will remain the only rational decision even if each individual
witness's testimony is not fully conclusive on its own. Even
if every one of the ten witnesses readily admitted that he or
she had some uncertainty about his or her testimony, by far
the best explanation of such an array of evidence all pointing
toward "not guilty" is that the defendant is in fact not guilty.

Perhaps your response to the chapters of this book has been
of this sort. You can see that there are various reasons pointing to the goodness of God, but you don't find every one of
them to be fully conclusive on its own. You continue to have
questions about whether God really values some of the things
we have claimed He values, or you have questions about
whether the possibility of suffering is really necessary for the
realization of some of these valuable things. If each chapter
is a witness, you are not sure whether some of the witnesses'
testimonies are conclusive on their own.

Here again, the multiplicity of reasons given is significant.
We have offered approximately ten perspectives through
which God is seen as good and trustworthy. Even if you continue to have questions about some of those perspectives, the
likelihood of there being so many apparent sightings of divine

goodness without one or more of them being reliable is very low. Actual divine goodness is the best explanation of such a diversity of testimony in God's favor.

The result is that even if you are not sure if the individual responses deal conclusively with the objection from suffering, it might still be the case that, when their testimonies are combined, they suggest conclusively and overwhelmingly that suffering does not negate the goodness of God.

This point is usually missed in discussions of the problem of suffering. Many assume that if they can cast doubt on each response individually, then they have discredited the responses taken as a whole. Not at all. Returning to our analogy, even if no individual testifier gives testimony that is indisputable, taken together, their testimonies would nevertheless be overwhelmingly convincing. Likewise, even if you judge that questions remain with respect to some of the individual responses given in favor of the goodness of God, you would still be rational in believing that the overall response is very likely to be successful.

When it comes to responding to the objection from suffering, more is better. First, because the more reasons God has for allowing suffering, the more likely it is that those reasons add up to a morally justifying reason overall. And, second, because the more potentially successful responses there are to the problem of suffering, the more likely it is that there is an actually successful response. For both of these reasons, the strongest response to the problem of suffering will be a cumulative response, and the variety of approaches offered within this book allows for such a response.

There is also a third and more practical reason that Ravi

and I decided to include a variety of responses to "Why suffering?" within the same book. Different words speak to us at different times. As Ravi has already alluded to, the words that made so much sense to C. S. Lewis when he penned them in *The Problem of Pain* in 1940 were not the words that he found helpful two decades later when his agony over his wife's death found expression in *A Grief Observed*.

We believe all of the responses recommended in this book have a good deal to be said for them intellectually, but you may find that the approach you found most compelling at this time may not be the one that helps at another time, and the approach that on this read seems irrelevant may on another day be of particular value.

A caring God would provide us with responses that are not only intellectually robust in some abstract sense, but that will cohere with our emotions day to day and year to year, in the variety of concrete challenges that we live through.

A Challenge for Everyone

Suffering is a challenge for everyone, and claiming atheism will do little to meet this challenge. It will do little to tell you how to wrestle with suffering in a world where so much of what you love and value depends on its possibility. It will do little to explain the objective evil of suffering and the response to it that goodness demands.

One thing we hope this book has shown is that it's okay to ask the hard questions about God. In fact, God welcomes that. There are few things better in life than discovering that someone really wants to know you—deeply. When they ask you real questions and aren't satisfied with superficial answers. When they want to understand even the parts of you that others find messy and complicated, the parts that others object to, avoid, run from altogether.

God gets that same delight when we strive to understand who He is and the ways He is at work in the world—when we say to Him, "Help me to understand You more. To the limited extent that I'm able, I want to know everything about You and the way You made the world and the reasons You have for the things that You do. I want to understand even the things that others find confusing and difficult about You, the things others attack, mock, make every effort to dismiss."

A tyrant doesn't want to be questioned; he wants only to be blindly followed. But a loving father welcomes questions. In the Bible, God is referred to as Father literally hundreds of times. Yes, He wants His children to follow His lead. But He also wants His children to begin to understand Him, and to love Him, and to trust Him.

And so in Christianity there is the freedom to wrestle with the question "God, *why* would you allow so much suffering?" The longest conversation in the entire Bible—the book of Job—concerns this very question. Jesus' earliest followers spent much of their time thinking about the hard questions of faith and discussing those questions with others. The "acts" that Jesus' disciples are described as performing in the book of the Bible called the Acts of the Apostles include "reasoning," "arguing," "persuading," "examining," "debating," "disputing," "explaining," "defending," "refuting," "convincing," and even "proving." All of those concepts are used in just that one book.

Christian faith is not a blind faith. Christian faith does not shy away from the tough questions.

For all of us, suffering is one of the toughest questions, and the more seriously you take suffering—indeed, the more seriously you take those who suffer—the more committed you will be to seeking a solution. We are all going to follow something. How is what you follow going to respond to suffering with integrity and with power? And how, in the end, will it be victorious over suffering?

A Challenge I Accepted

For years I had little idea how to answer these questions regarding suffering. I was not a Christian when I showed up at Princeton University as a freshman. It's not so much that I didn't believe in God, but more that I hid in my heart what Nietzsche was audacious enough to put to paper: "If there were gods, how could I stand not to be a god!"[5]

I accepted a challenge from a friend to test my assumptions about Christianity by reading the Gospels—four records of Jesus' life—and I began to argue my way through them. I would cross things out and add things and write "BS" in the margins (not, as some assumed, to denote great passages for "Bible Study").

In my arrogance I thought I was teaching God a thing or two, and yet all the while I was coming to admire the person of Jesus. I began to think that He had lived the most beautiful life ever lived. I began to think that He, above all others, was a person worth following.

But I just didn't think it could be true! I didn't think there could be actual evidence for Christianity. I didn't think it could be intellectually defended, and, for me, that was a must. I was studying philosophy; I was committed to truth. It was essential to me to be able to defend my beliefs. I couldn't just forsake my mind to take some blind leap of faith.

But as I continued reading, I kept seeing that far from praising blind faith, the Bible praised those who "examined" the evidence every day to determine if what they were being told was true (Acts 17:11). And so I began to look into the evidence and the arguments. I can recall reasoning that if God really made me, and if He made me with my mind, then He would want me to use my mind to seek Him, and He would ensure that a sincere intellectual search would point in His direction.

I couldn't believe what I found. I couldn't believe how strong the intellectual case for the Christian faith is. I encountered many arguments for God's existence that were compelling, probably as many as fifteen or so, and I hope to write about these arguments in the future. As with responses to the problem of suffering, I again found that more is better; the multiplicity of arguments for God's existence made the overall case much stronger than I had ever imagined it could be.

One of the arguments I found most compelling concerned the supposed resurrection of Jesus from the dead. It had never crossed my mind that there could be historical evidence for such a thing; I was astounded by how persuasive I found the arguments.

The most influential British philosopher of religion of the last half century is Richard Swinburne. Before retiring he held the most senior post in philosophy of religion at the University of Oxford. In 2003, Swinburne published a book titled *The Resurrection of God Incarnate*, and in that book he concludes that on the available evidence today, it is 97 percent probable that Jesus Christ miraculously rose from the dead, proving that He is the God He claimed to be.[6]

Of course, Swinburne recognizes that we can't take the exact percentage too seriously; it is meant to be only an estimation. Nevertheless, the fact that someone of Swinburne's intellectual credibility can make that claim in print, have it published by Oxford University Press, and then ably defend it at top academic conferences all around the world symbolizes just how strong the intellectual case for Christianity is.

I was actually reading a defense of the resurrection when I first trusted Jesus. As I closed the book's back cover, I simply knew—with a conviction that transcended all of my imperfect reasoning and theorizing and calculating—that Jesus was the God He claimed to be, that He loved me, that He had saved me, that He wanted me to live with Him in the days ahead.

It wasn't just that my mind was persuaded by what I had read; my heart was finally in a place of desiring to know God. And God gave me that gift. I was alone in my dorm room—122 Joline Hall—but I exclaimed out loud, "This really happened!"

What Keeps Us from God?

We hope one of the things you'll take from this book is that there is not a conflict between Christian faith and reason. God gave us our hearts and our minds, and He wants us to use both in our pursuit of Him.

If we think it is intellectual arguments that keep us from God, then we may not be dealing with the arguments at the highest level. There is more than enough evidence to take a rational leap of faith and trust in Christ. What keeps us from God is often not our minds but the rest of us. Sometimes we're too lazy to care. Sometimes we're too distracted to care. Sometimes, if we're honest, we simply like being our own gods.

Do you want to know God?

If you were given sufficient evidence to believe in God, would you then follow Him?

When you read those questions, what is your instinctual answer? Because all of these debates are merely academic unless you can answer yes to those questions. Only then does the evidence really matter. Only then will you know the fulfillment of God's promise:

You will seek me and find me when you seek me with all your heart. (Jeremiah 29:13)

Sometimes we're so quick to say God is not there, especially when we are suffering. Have we asked Him to be there? We all know that when we try to push into someone else's life, and in particular into their suffering, it only makes things worse.

God wouldn't push His way into my life, but when I invited Him, He was there. When I prayed an agnostic's prayer—"God, I don't know if I'm talking to anyone, but if I am, I'd really like to know about it"—I found that God answered. When I said, "I'm sorry for the ways I've wronged You and others," I knew God's full forgiveness—forgiveness without limit or qualification. When I said, "Yes, God, I will trust You with my life, even though I still have many questions and I don't have it all figured out," for the first time I knew God—not *about* God, but God Himself.

That's some of my story. One day, after we're all gone, someone will be telling each of our stories. And after they get past the funny moments and the embarrassing tales, what will they say? Will they say you were one who caused suffering? Or will they say you were one who was willing to suffer for the sake of others?

I hope what they will say about me is that I chose to follow Jesus, and to honor His life—a life centered on an unconditional commitment not to cause suffering but to help others through it, no matter the cost:

> This is how we know what love is: Jesus Christ laid down his life for us. And we ought to lay down our lives for our brothers and sisters. (1 John 3:16)

At its core, this is what it means to be a Christian—to place your trust in a person who was willing to lay down His life to defeat the sin and suffering in your life, and to commit to following Jesus by being willing to lay down your life for others.

Maybe you thought suffering was a knockdown objection to Christian faith. Maybe now you see that is not the case. If God can be loving and good even amid suffering, then perhaps He can be trusted with the rest of life as well.

That commitment of trust can be made with simple but sincere words:

> "I'm sorry."
> "Thank You."

I'm sorry, God, for the suffering I've caused—the suffering I've caused You, the suffering I've caused others, the suffering I've caused myself.

Thank You for not giving up on me. Thank You for being willing to make even the greatest sacrifice on my behalf, and in doing so proving that when I know pain in my heart and tears from my eyes, when the only words I can manage are "Why suffering?," You hear and You respond.

Acknowledgments

Ravi Zacharias

It has been an honor to work with Vince Vitale on this book. We wrote the chapters separately and he took on the arduous task of pulling them together. My gratitude to him.

So many others have made this effort possible:

Working with Joey Paul and gaining from his years of experience and firsthand knowledge of styles and readability was a valuable resource for me. He is a very dear friend to us and we treasure his friendship.

My research assistant, Danielle DuRant, does the work of chasing down references and is a wise advisor on the content. She knows my material better than anyone else.

There is only one exception to that, and that is my wife, Margie. Travel is a hazard of my trade and when writing demands even further absence, she has never complained. As always, she is also my editor and on all matters has the last word. Yes, I say that with a smile.

My heartfelt thanks to the decision makers at Hachette. Without their trust and investment, none of this would be possible.

I would be missing the most important people of all if I didn't thank those who I have known in life that have suffered much and have, with grace and humility, shared their struggle and triumph. They are really the wise of the earth and it is because of them these arguments have been embodied. That's how this book has taken shape.

Vince Vitale

I cannot say enough about the generosity that Ravi, the Zacharias family, and the RZIM team have shown to me and my wife, Jo. They have consistently found ways to trust us beyond any trust that we have earned. We thank God for their friendship and partnership.

Ravi in particular has modeled to me that humility must be at the center of every success. Never have I met a person who is so successful in what they do, and yet so humble. He has set an example of a lifetime of faithful ministry that points to Jesus Christ.

Joey Paul believed in this project from the start, and saw it through with tremendous discernment and care. Martin Smith's meticulous and incisive comments on a penultimate draft were invaluable. I am deeply grateful to them both.

Two people who have influenced nearly every page I have written are my uncle John and my cousin Charles. Through their disabilities, they were able to give to our family as much as anyone. Their lives were my first glimpse that there could be hopeful responses to "Why suffering?"

My deepest gratitude is to my wife. Amidst her own busy schedule, Jo gave countless hours to this project, poring over the chapters and helping me to make decisions both big and painstakingly small. It is hard to imagine anyone being more patient with me or more willing to give of themselves for me. In this she unwaveringly directs me to God, who deserves the greatest acknowledgment for having provided the hope most worth writing about.

Notes

Chapter 1: The Question

1. J. L. Mackie, "Evil and Omnipotence," *Mind*, n.s., 64, no. 254 (April 1955): 200. Available online at http://www.ditext.com/mackie/evil.html.
2. Song from *Shree 420*, directed by Raj Kapoor (1955; India: R. K. Films Ltd.). See http://en.wikipedia.org/wiki/Mera_Joota_hai_Japani.
3. "Daniel Dennett and Jesus Christ," by Nick Spencer, *Theos*, http://www.theosthinktank.co.uk/comment/2013/07/04/daniel -dennett-and-jesus. Originally published under the title "Mounting Disbelief" in *Third Way* magazine (July 2013); access by subscription only.
4. Susan Shatto and Marion Shaw, eds., *Tennyson: In Memoriam* (Oxford: Clarendon Press, 1982), 80.
5. G. K. Chesterton, *Orthodoxy* (New York: John Lane, 1908), 104.
6. See an excerpt of Antony Flew, "Theology and Falsification," in *Reason and Responsibility: Readings in Some Basic Problems of Philosophy*, ed. Joel Feinberg and Russ Shafer-Landau (Belmont, CA: Dickenson, 1968), 48–49. Accessed online on March 29, 2014, at http://www2.sunysuffolk.edu/pecorip/SCCCWEB/ETEXTS/PHIL_of_RELIGION_TEXT/CHAPTER_8_LANGUAGE/Theology-and-Falsification.htm.
7. John H. Frame, "God and Biblical Language: Transcendence and Immanence," in *God's Inerrant Word: An International Symposium on the Trustworthiness of Scripture*, ed. J. W. Montgomery (Minneapolis: Bethany Fellowship, 1974), 171.
8. Alvin C. Plantinga, *God, Freedom, and Evil* (Grand Rapids, MI: Eerdmans, 1977), 63–64.

9. John S. Feinberg, "A Journey in Suffering: Personal Reflections on the Religious Problem of Evil," in *Suffering and the Goodness of God*, ed. Christopher W. Morgan and Robert A. Peterson (Wheaton, IL: Crossway, 2008), 219.

10. Ibid.

Chapter 2: A Response of Freedom

1. John C. Lennox, *Seven Days That Divide the World: The Beginning According to Genesis and Science* (Grand Rapids, MI: Zondervan, 2011).

2. Chandra Wickramasinghe, "Prof. Chandra Wickramasinghe—the man who asserted: 'Life did not start here on earth but in space,' has retired," *Asian Tribune*, n.p., n.d., accessed online in April 2014 at http://www.asiantribune.com/index.php?q=node/2788.

3. Henry Wadsworth Longfellow, "A Psalm of Life," in *The Oxford Anthology of American Literature*, vol. 1, ed. William Rose Benét and Norman Holmes Pearson (New York: Oxford University Press, 1954), 567.

4. Robert W. Yarbrough, "Christ and the Crocodiles: Suffering and the Goodness of God in Contemporary Perspective," in *Suffering and the Goodness of God*, ed. Christopher W. Morgan and Robert A. Peterson (Wheaton, IL: Crossway, 2008), 23–46.

5. G. K. Chesterton, *Orthodoxy* (New York: John Lane, 1908), 50.

6. Søren Kierkegaard, *Either/Or, Part 1*, ed. and trans. Howard V. Hong and Edna H. Hong (Princeton, NJ: Princeton University Press, 1987), 31.

7. James Shane, *The Laws of Life* (Maitland, FL: Xulon Press, 2002), 649.

8. Fyodor Dostoevsky, *The Brothers Karamazov*, trans. Constance Garnett (New York: Signet Classic, 1999), 312. Accessed online on March 30, 2014, at http://www.online-literature.com/dostoevsky/brothers_karamazov/41/.

9. Saint Augustine, *Confessions*, trans. Henry Chadwick (New York: Oxford University Press, 2008), 3.

10. Calvin Miller, *Spirit, Word, and Story: A Philosophy of Preaching* (Nashville: Word, 1989), 50.

11. Malcolm Muggeridge, *A Twentieth Century Testimony* (Nashville: Thomas Nelson, 1978), 27.

12. James S. Stewart, *The Strong Name* (Edinburgh: T. & T. Clark, 1940), 55.

Chapter 3: A Response of Grace

1. The American Chesterton Society is inclined to think this anecdote is true; however, documentary evidence of it has not been found. In any case, it is a poignant example of recognizing the need to look within the human heart to make sense of the world around us.

2. In the original Hebrew, the names are חוה ("Eve") and יהוה ("Yahweh"). I do not mean to imply here that Adam knew the name "Yahweh" when he named Eve.

3. Gottfried Wilhelm Leibniz, "The Confession of a Philosopher," in *G. W. Leibniz, Confessio philosophi: Papers Concerning the Problem of Evil, 1671–1678*, ed. and trans. Robert C. Sleigh Jr. (New Haven, CT: Yale University Press, 2005), 104–7.

4. See Robert M. Adams, "Must God Create the Best?," *Philosophical Review* 81, no. 3 (1972): 317–32; and Adams, "Existence, Self-Interest, and the Problem of Evil," in *The Virtue of Faith and Other Essays in Philosophical Theology* (Oxford: Oxford University Press, 1987), 65–76.

5. A related point is made in 2 Peter 3, especially verses 8–9: "But do not forget this one thing, dear friends: With the Lord a day is like a thousand years, and a thousand years are like a day. The Lord is not slow in keeping his promise, as some understand slowness. Instead he is patient with you, not wanting anyone to perish, but everyone to come to repentance."

6. Leibniz makes a similar point when he considers a half-noble son who is "irritated with his father because he had married a woman unequal in rank . . . not thinking that if his father had married someone else, not he, but some other man, would have come into the world." Leibniz, "The Confession of a Philosopher," 107.

7. Leibniz considers a related question in "The Confession of a Philosopher," 104–7.

8. When I wrote to James's mom to ask if she would be happy for me to share her story, she replied, "That is perfectly fine with me. I can see that day so well in my mind . . . Considering what was going on in my life and how I felt and looked I definitely didn't expect anyone to like me let alone fall in love with me . . . We were both so broken and beaten down at that time and still trying to get through each day . . .

God truly took me from my lowest point of brokenness and lifted me up and blessed me beyond what I could have imagined. He continues to bless me every day even though I don't deserve it. Only by His grace."

9. I am reminded here of King David's words: "What are human beings that you are mindful of them, mortals that you care for them?" (Psalm 8:4 NRSV).

10. For a classic presentation of a soul-making approach, see John Hick, *Evil and the God of Love*, 2d ed. (London: Macmillan, 1977).

11. For van Inwagen's discussion of this theory, see his "The Magnitude, Duration and Distribution of Evil: A Theodicy," *Philosophical Topics* 16, no. 2 (1988); and *The Problem of Evil: The Gifford Lectures Delivered in the University of St. Andrews in 2003* (New York: Oxford University Press, 2006).

12. For those with an interest in how the response of this chapter relates to different philosophical views about free will, let me say a bit more. There are three primary ways of thinking about free will, and the response I have outlined can work on all three of them.

If one believes in determinism (whereby free will either does not exist or is understood in such a way that it is compatible with God's determining all events), then God can arrange human history down to the smallest detail, and thereby aim for specific persons to come to exist. If one believes in Molinism (whereby human persons have undetermined free will but God knows how every possible person would freely act in any possible circumstances He can put them in), then again God can aim for specific persons; He can do so by deciding which circumstances to place free persons into. If one holds to non-Molinist libertarian free will (whereby human persons have undetermined free will but God does not know with certainty how people would freely act in various circumstances), then we have a slightly more complicated case.

In this third case, God could still have full knowledge of the future from an atemporal perspective. Metaphorically, we could think of God as seeing the continuum of time like a road stretched out before Him. When He looks down the road at a portion of time that is future with respect to us, He timelessly knows the free actions that happen at that time. But He has this knowledge because He is seeing what is *actually* freely being done at that time, not because He has caused it to be the case or controlled the outcome in advance. On this view, God's knowledge of free actions is logically posterior to the actions themselves; the actual occurrence of the free actions explains God's knowledge of them. Therefore, even though from an atemporal perspective God may always know which free actions will occur, and which specific persons will as a result come to exist, this knowledge could not be used by God to aim for specific individuals. Logically, His knowledge of who will come to exist depends on His knowledge of what free actions will be performed. However, His knowledge of what free actions will be performed depends on the performers of those actions already existing, and it would be incoherent to use knowledge that depends on people already existing in order to determine that those people will in fact exist.

But even on this third approach to free will, one could still hold that even if God does not arrange the free decisions relevant to procreation history with precision sufficient for aiming for specific persons to come to exist, He would still have enough control over the unfolding of the universe to aim for the being-type of human persons generally. And, in fact, this would make divine creation even more analogous to human procreation. Human parents don't procreate knowing the *specific* child they will bring into existence. They decide to bring into existence a being of a certain type—a human person—and they do so with a determination to love whichever specific individual they wind up bringing into the world. Despite aiming for a being-type rather than a specific individual in procreating, there still seems to be a significant sense in which human parents can procreate out of love for their future children. Likewise, even on non-Molinist libertarian assumptions about free will, God can create and sustain the universe out of love for the human persons who come to exist.

Moreover, God would have several advantages over human procreators even on this third approach to free will. Whereas human parents have only a very vague sense of whom they might wind up with when procreating, God knits each person together in their mother's womb. And, as previously noted, whereas human parents are often helpless to overcome suffering in a child's life, God can offer every person an eternal life of extraordinary value.

13. Elsewhere I name this response to the problem of suffering "Non-Identity Theodicy." *Theodicy* (taken from the Greek words *theos* ["God"] and *dikē* ["justice"]) is the word Leibniz coined for a theory about why God permits evil; "Non-Identity" signifies that in a significantly different world, those who came to exist would not be identical to those who came to exist in the actual world.

Chapter 4: A Response at the Cross

1. Friedrich W. Nietzsche, *The Birth of Tragedy and the Genealogy of Morals*, trans. Francis Golffing (Garden City, NY: Doubleday, 1956), 30.
2. Richard Dawkins, *The God Delusion* (London: Bantam Press, 2006), 252–53.
3. In what follows I focus primarily on how Jesus' incarnation, suffering, and death bear on the problem of suffering. For those who wish to explore the meaning of Jesus' death in greater detail, John Stott's *The Cross of Christ*—which I reference below—would be an excellent place to start.
4. John R. W. Stott, *The Cross of Christ* (Downers Grove, IL: InterVarsity, 2006), 387.
5. Compare Matthew 5:27–28.
6. Compare Matthew 5:21–22. See also 1 John 3:15.
7. Jesus took on not only human flesh but a full human nature. Compare John 1:14; Philippians 2:5–8; and Hebrews 2:5–18 (especially verses 14 and 17).
8. Ephesians 2:10: "For we are God's masterpiece. He has created us anew in Christ Jesus, so we can do the good things he planned for us long ago" (NLT).
9. Eleonore Stump, *Wandering in Darkness: Narrative and the Problem of Suffering* (Oxford: Clarendon, 2010), 171, cf. 397.

Chapter 5: Other Responses on Offer: Buddhism, Islam, Naturalism

1. Andrew Fletcher, quoted in Harold A. Bosley, *Sermons on the Psalms* (New York: Harper and Row, 1965), 11.
2. "Question," words and Music by Justin Hayward. © Copyright 1970 (Renewed) Tyler Music Ltd., London, England. TRO–Essex Music International, Inc., New York, controls all publication rights for the U.S.A. and Canada. Used by Permission.

3. C. S. Lewis, *The Problem of Pain* (London: Centenary Press, 1940).

4. Gabriel Marcel, *The Philosophy of Existentialism*, trans. Manya Harari (New York: Carol Publishing, 1995), 19.

5. Peter Kreeft, *Making Sense Out of Suffering* (Ann Arbor, MI: Servant, 1986), 51.

6. David Hume, *Dialogues Concerning Natural Religion*, part 10, ed. Henry D. Aiken (New York: Hafner, 1963), 64.

7. Source unknown.

8. Yasmin Mogahed, *Reclaim Your Heart: Personal Insights on Breaking Free from Life's Shackles* (San Clemente, CA: FB Publishing, 2012).

9. Al-Imam al-'Izz bin Abdi-s-Salam, *Trials and Tribulations: Wisdom and Benefits* (London: Daar us-sunnah Publishers, 2004), 23–24n21.

10. Readers may find this material online: Yasmin Mogahed, "Why Do People Have To Leave Each Other?" part 1 (March 29, 2011), at http://www.suhaibwebb.com/personaldvlpt/character/why-do-people-have-to-leave-each-other.

11. As quoted in Salam, *Trials and Tribulations*, 48.

12. Ibid., 50.

13. Ibid., 51, 59.

14. Yasmin Mogahed, "Attachments: Emptying the Vessel," December 7, 2010, http://www.suhaibwebb.com/personaldvlpt/attachments-emptying-the-vessel.

15. Mogahed, *Reclaim Your Heart*, 64.

16. See C. S. Lewis, *Mere Christianity* (London: HarperCollins, 2002), 69–75.

17. See Debarshi Dasgupta, "Frozen, Framed," *Outlook* (August 26, 2013), 23, available online at http://www.outlookindia.com/article.aspx?287393. The article is about filmmaker Kumar Krishnamsetty.

18. Ibid.

Chapter 6: A Response from Morality

1. J. L. Mackie, quoted in J. P. Moreland, "Reflections on Meaning in Life without God," *Trinity Journal*, n.s., 9, no. 1 (1988): 14.

2. Kai Nielsen, "Why Should I Be Moral? Revisited," *American Philosophical Quarterly* 21, no. 1 (1984): 90.

3. Richard Dawkins, *Out of Eden* (New York: Basic Books, 1992), 133.

4. Hobart Mowrer, " 'Sin': The Lesser of Two Evils," *American Psychologist* 15, no. 5 (1960): 303.

5. Richard Dawkins argues that religion is a "mental virus of faith" in his essay "Viruses of the Mind," *Free Inquiry* (Summer 1993): 34–41.

6. G. K. Chesterton, *Orthodoxy* (New York: John Lane, 1908), 73–74.

7. Edward O. Wilson, *Sociobiology: The New Synthesis* (Cambridge, MA: Harvard University Press, 1975), 562, emphasis added.

8. Daniel Goleman, *Emotional Intelligence: Why It Can Matter More Than IQ* (New York: Bantam, 1995).

9. Nielsen, "Why Should I Be Moral?," 90.

10. Bertrand Russell and F. C. Copleston, "A Debate on the Existence of God," in *Bertrand Russell on God and Religion*, ed. Al Seckel (Amherst, NY: Prometheus Books, 1986), 138–39.

11. This is called the "Rule According to Higher Law": "Political leaders assert that all written laws must conform with universal principles of morality, fairness, and justice. These leaders argue that as a necessary corollary to the axiom that 'no one is above the law' the rule of law requires that the government treat all persons equally under the law… These unwritten principles of equality, autonomy, dignity, and respect are said to transcend ordinary written laws that are enacted by government. Sometimes known as Natural Law or higher law theory, such unwritten and universal principles were invoked by the Allied powers during the Nuremberg trials to overcome the defense asserted by the Nazi leaders." Accessed on April 15, 2014, at http://legal-dictionary.thefreedictionary.com/Rule+According+to+Higher+Law. See also Affirmation of the Principles of International Law recognized by the Charter of the Nürnberg Tribunal General Assembly resolution 95 (I), New York, 11 December 1946, accessed online on April 15, 2014, at http://www.un.org/law/avl.

12. Jean-Paul Sartre, *Being and Nothingness* (New York: Pocket Books, 1984), 478.

13. Steve Turner, "Chance," in *Nice and Nasty* (Manchester: Razor Books, 1980), 54. Permission to reprint granted by the author.

14. George MacDonald, as quoted in "Words and Truths, Part II," *British Friend* 7, vol. 1 (July 5, 1892): 157. Available online at http://books.google.com/books?id=vDMrAAAAYAAJ&dq=george%20macdonald%201892%20british%20friend&pg=PA157#v=onepage&q&f=false.

Chapter 7: A Response of Hope

1. Aldous Huxley, "Variations on a Baroque Tomb," in *Themes and Variations* (London: Chatto and Windus, 1950), 164.
2. Søren Kierkegaard, Howard V. Hong, Edna H. Hong, and Gregor Malantschuk, *Søren Kierkegaard's Journals and Papers: 1829–1848* (Bloomington: Indiana University Press, 1978), JP 5, 6132.
3. Compare Romans 8:18–22.
4. Dr. James Lee expressed this to me in e-mail correspondence.
5. Blaise Pascal speaks to this idea in a number of insightful ways in his *Pensées* (1669)—posthumously published notes that he was preparing for an extensive defense of Christianity.
6. This idea is taken from Peter van Inwagen, "The Magnitude, Duration, and Distribution of Evil: A Theodicy," *Philosophical Topics* 16 (1988): 161–87. There he suggests that "when God's plan of Atonement comes to fruition, there will never again be undeserved suffering or any other sort of evil. The 'age of evil' will eventually be remembered as a sort of transient 'flicker' at the very beginning of human history" (165).
7. This analogy is inspired by one discussed by Eleonore Stump in *Wandering in Darkness: Narrative and the Problem of Suffering* (Oxford: Clarendon Press, 2010), 17–18.
8. I take this suggestion from Eleonore Stump, *Wandering in Darkness*, 466.
9. This quotation is shared by the narrator in *Billy Graham: God's Ambassador*, directed by Michael Merriman (Spring House, 2006), DVD. It is most likely an adaptation of words spoken by D. L. Moody: "Some day you will read in the papers that D. L. Moody, of East Northfield, is dead. Don't you believe a word of it! At that moment I shall be more alive than I am now. I shall have gone up higher, that is all—out of this old clay tenement into a house that is immortal; a body that death cannot touch, that sin cannot taint, a body fashioned like unto His glorious body. I was born of the flesh in 1837. I was born of the Spirit in 1856. That which is born of the flesh may die. That which is born of the Spirit will live for ever." William R. Moody, *The Life of Dwight L. Moody* (Kilmarnock, Scotland: John Ritchie, 1900), 475.

Chapter 8: God's Manifold Responses

1. Timothy Keller, *The Reason for God: Belief in an Age of Skepticism* (New York: Penguin, 2008), 25.

2. This line of thought is termed "Skeptical Theism" because it recommends that we be skeptical of the assumption that we should expect to know God's reasons for allowing evil and suffering. In an important article published in 1979 ("The Problem of Evil and Some Varieties of Atheism," *American Philosophical Quarterly* 16, no. 4, 335–41), William Rowe argued that because we can't imagine what good reasons there could be for God to allow some of the evils of this world, we should conclude that there probably are no good reasons. These types of arguments have come to be known as "noseeum" inferences in the literature. I "no see um"; therefore, "there ain't 'em." I don't see a reason; therefore, there probably is not a reason. Stephen Wykstra responded to Rowe in a highly influential article ("The Humean Obstacle to Evidential Arguments from Suffering: On Avoiding the Evils of 'Appearance,'" *International Journal for Philosophy of Religion* 16, no. 2 [1984]: 73–93) that argued that noseeum inferences are sometimes bad inferences, and in particular that not seeing God's reasons is not good reason to conclude that He doesn't have any.

3. Compare Romans 11:34 and Isaiah 40:13.

4. This does not imply that love will be impossible in heaven. In heaven we will treat one another lovingly not because we lack the power to do otherwise but because our union with God will confirm in us such a genuine care for one another that we will freely act out of love.

5. Friedrich W. Nietzsche, *Thus Spoke Zarathustra: A Book for All and None*, ed. Adrian Del Caro and Robert B. Pippin (Cambridge: Cambridge University Press, 2006), 75.

6. Richard Swinburne, *The Resurrection of God Incarnate* (Oxford: Oxford University Press, 2003), 214.